JOHN BUNYAN

John Bunyan

Allegory and Imagination

E. Beatrice Batson

CROOM HELM   London & Canberra
BARNES & NOBLE BOOKS   Totowa, New Jersey

© 1984 E. Beatrice Batson
Croom Helm Ltd, Provident House, Burrell Row,
Beckenham, Kent BR3 1AT

Croom Helm Australia, PO Box 391,
Manuka, ACT 2603, Australia

British Library Cataloguing in Publication Data

Batson, E. Beatrice
  John Bunyan.
    1. Bunyan. — Criticism and interpretation
    I. Title
    828'.408   PR3332
  ISBN 0-7099-3227-8

First published in the USA 1984 by
Barnes & Noble Books
81 Adams Drive
Totowa, New Jersey 07512

Library of Congress Cataloging in Publication Data

Batson, E. Beatrice.
  John Bunyan.
  Bibliography: p.
  Includes index.
  1. Bunyan, John, 1628-1688 — Criticism and interpreta-
tion. 2. Bunyan, John, 1628-1688 — Allegory and symbolism.
3. Theology in literature. 4. Scholasticism in literature.
I. Title.
PR3332.B35   1984   828'.407   83-21341
ISBN 0-389-20442-0

Printed and bound in Great Britain

CONTENTS

In memory of my mother and my father

PREFACE

The heritage of the Puritan tradition to literary study is enormously significant. Although the contributions of the tradition are by no means limited to literature, I shall limit this study to the literary ways of one Puritan writer, John Bunyan. What this Bedfordshire tinker and preacher does to shape his writings into literary form shows the work of a conscious artist. Certainly one might write with interest on his theology and preaching as well as on his social and political concerns, but this study is an attempt to direct attention to the literary features of the various genres in which he writes, including his sermon-treatises.

The introductory chapter attempts to show not only Bunyan's appreciation for and understanding of imaginative literature but also to demonstrate that his concern with the moral or didactic quality of literature is shared by numerous reputable writers. What also becomes evident is that a moral or theological focus is no enemy of imaginative literature. Following the introductory chapter, the book concentrates on literary qualities which shape his autobiography, the allegories, the Dialogues, the Emblems, and sermon-treatises.

To the staff of the following libraries I express appreciation for making available various editions and original copies of John Bunyan's works: the British Museum; the Bodleian, Oxford; the Huntington, San Marino, California; the Newberry, Chicago; and the Wheaton College Library, Wheaton, Illinois. My thanks also go to the Curator of the Bunyan Museum, Bedford, for showing me the collection of Bunyan memorabilia, a reminder of the earnest spirit and creative energy of the tinker and the preacher.

I wish also to thank Miss Ivy Olson of the Wheaton College Library who graciously assisted in locating numerous articles not readily accessible. To Miss Nancy Arnesen, a busy graduate student in English literature, and to Mrs Joyce Anderson, Secretary of the Department of English at Wheaton College, I offer my deep appreciation for giving unstintingly of their time to type the manuscript. My thanks also go to Nancy Arnesen for her capable assistance in the editing of the manuscript.

1 INTRODUCTION

The acceptance of John Bunyan as a literary figure has been a matter of growth as slow as the popularity of *The Pilgrim's Progress* had been immediate. C.H. Firth suggested that Addison cited Bunyan as proof that even despicable writers had their admirers; Young compared his prose to D'urfey's poetry, and when Cowper praised him he apologised for his tributes by refusing to name him, 'lest so despised a name / should move a sneer at thy deserved fame.' Before the end of the eighteenth century other literary names had begun to praise the works of John Bunyan.

Swift wrote that he had been entertained and more confirmed by a few pages in *The Pilgrim's Progress* than by a long discussion upon the will and intellect. Johnson compared passages in it to Spenser and Dante and believed that it had great merit both for invention and imagination. In 1830, with the publication of Southey's edition of *The Pilgrim's Progress* followed by Macaulay's essay, men of letters had come closer to accepting John Bunyan as a literary author.[1] Coleridge considered *The Pilgrim's Progress* to be one of the few books that might be read repeatedly with a new and different pleasure and admitted that he had read it once as a theologian, once as a poet, and once 'with devotional feelings', and each time with exquisite delight. George Eliot expressed her appreciation in the statement: 'I am reading old Bunyan again, after the long lapse of years, and am profoundly struck with the true genius manifested in the simple, vigorous rhythmic style.'[2] Admittedly, praise for the literary merit was sporadic, but it was, nevertheless, evident.

In the twentieth century, Charles Angell Bradford declares that 'the allegory of allegories of the English-speaking race is Bunyan's *Pilgrim's Progress*';[3] Clifford Kent Wright applauds the raciness of its narrative and the graphic reality of its portraiture and contends that 'as in the beginning of the *Odyssey*, the opening scene of *Hamlet*, and the first page of *The Divine Comedy*, the reader's attention is gripped at the outset',[4] while Angus Fletcher speaks of the high degree of emotive ambivalence in allegorical literature and states that it is sometimes 'synonymous with the names of authors — Swift, Bunyan, Melville, Kafka'.[5] Although other works have

1

received some commendation,[6] it is *The Pilgrim's Progress*, and perhaps justifiably so, that receives greatest tribute as an outstanding imaginative work.

But with increasing praise extended to his masterpiece, critics still seem to raise questions about John Bunyan as an artist. Typical attitudes or opinions are: 'an Artist in Spite of Himself ',[7] or a 'true artist, though he knew nothing of the rules, and was not aware that he was an artist at all',[8] or a 'typical mechanick preacher' whose writings 'owe their nature both to the social, economic, and sectarian condition of their author and to the literary convention of a numerous company of mechanicks',[9] or the author of an autobiography, unexcelled for its keen 'psychological insight',[10] or a writer with the 'natural instinct' to express 'each change of feeling, each vicissitude in his spiritual conflict, in figurative or metaphorical form',[11] or one who 'worked without any critical understanding of the potentialities of the various forms he employed'.[12] Henri Talon, whose splendid interpretative work includes numerous references to Bunyan's artistic power, writes: 'He felt instinctively that eloquence would be a lapse of taste as well as a kind of profanation' and adds, 'the homely image is not sought out and as it were cultivated, but now and then it springs naturally from the pen of this man of the people.'[13]

Critics of Bunyan's writings, therefore, largely fall into two camps: those who suggest that when he shows artistic strength, he does it 'unconsciously' or 'in spite of himself' and those who attempt to explain his writings as illustrations of his Bedford-Nonconformist background, thus studying his works for other than literary reasons.

That Bunyan had read one scholarly work in literary criticism, or the celebration of the imagination in *A Midsummer Night's Dream*, or the 'mirror up to nature' speech of *Hamlet* is highly improbable. Yet there is much evidence that he thought often on the nature of metaphorical language; and contrary to the judgement of some, he apparently thought of himself not only as a moral teacher and preacher but also as an author of imaginative literature. To hint that John Bunyan had no interest in the didactic quality of his writing is erroneous; to suggest that there are not numerous authors of kindred mind is equally fallacious. As D.W. Robertson Jr. aptly affirms, 'it is not difficult to cite evidence to show that during the Middle Ages and, indeed, well into the Renaissance, figurative expression in both literary and visual art was designed to lead the mind through exercise to a spiritual understanding.'[14]

The underlying principle of Robertson's position is a theory of literature expounded in Augustine's *On Christian Doctrine* (to which Robertson frequently refers). To put the matter at its simplest, the theory bears a close relationship to the statement of Paul, 'the letter kills, but the spirit gives life' (2 Cor. 3:6). Literature has two parts, the literal and the figurative, which may include several meanings. In order to interpret and understand correctly, one must resist the interpretative pressure of the exclusively literal in favour of something (doctrinal truths), or Someone (the persons of the Trinity). As Bernard F. Huppé discerningly perceives:

> For Augustine — and his tradition — the intention of literature was to promote the 'reign of charity'; that is, literature like all the other activities of man, was considered truly functional only as it contributed to God's purpose, unfolded in the New Law wherein man's whole duty is expressed.[15]

In brief, literature, especially through figurative expression, offers an opportunity to know the invisible God and to discern his purposes through 'the things that are made' or that are visible.

It is wise, however, to permit Augustine to speak for himself. It is his firm belief that the enigma or the obscurity of a figurative expression is ordained by God to stimulate a desire to learn, to prevail over pride by work and thought, and 'to prevent the mind from disdaining a thing too easily grasped'.[16] He clearly states his position:

> But why it seems sweeter to me than if no such similitude were offered in the divine books, since the thing perceived is the same, is difficult to say . . . For the present, however, no one doubts that things are perceived more readily through similitudes than that what is sought with difficulty is discovered with more pleasure. Those who do not find what they seek directly stated labor in hunger; those who do not seek because they have what they wish at once frequently become indolent in disdain . . . Thus the Holy Spirit has magnificently and wholesomely modulated the Holy Scriptures so that the more open places present themselves to hunger and the more obscure places may deter a disdainful pleasure.[17]

For Augustine, then, literature enhances spiritual understanding which is the 'location of the referents suggested by figures';[18] moreover, the beauty of literature stems from its enhancement of the reader's understanding of something beyond 'the thing itself', the merely visible or literal.

Other writers reflect the literary theory established in Augustine's *On Christian Doctrine*. When Dante says in his alleged Epistle to Can Grande della Scalla that the purpose of the *Commedia* is moral, he is echoing the Augustinian dictum and is suggesting that he employs the journey metaphor to show the subtlest theological, metaphysical, and epistemological distinctions. Similarly, Boccaccio, in enjoining readers to 'unwind difficult involutions' of poetry, suggests that there is a double movement in literature, that of the literal narrative and the movement of understanding on another level. 'If one way does not lead to the desired meaning,' he says, 'take another; if obstacles arise, then still another; until, if your strength holds out, you will find that clear which at first looked dark. For we are forbidden by divine command to give that which is holy to dogs, or to cast pearls before swine.'[19]

Chaucer shows no lack of acquaintance with the Augustinian position on literature. That he left no explicit statements on aesthetics we readily admit, but in his 'Retractions' at the end of 'The Parson's Tale', he quotes from Paul, 'Al that is writen is writen for oure doctrine,' and adds, 'and that is myn entente.' If one is less than satisfied with the statement, a thoughtful reading of 'The Parson's Tale' itself, as well as other works, will reveal the familiarity with the aesthetic principles thus far discussed.[20]

In the Renaissance era, the stance of Sir Philip Sidney bears similarities to his predecessors. He thinks of a writer as a 'maker' — a maker of an imaginative construct, and the writer 'makes' and invents for a purpose. Taking from the Roman poet Horace the view that the poet both delights and teaches, Sidney proceeds to show that the poets

> indeede doo meerely make to imitate, and imitate both to delight and teach, and delight to moue men to take that goodnes in hande, which without delight they would flye as from a stranger: And teach, to make them know that goodnes whereunto they are mooued, which being the noblest scope to which ever any learning was directed . . .[21]

He further says: ' . . . it is that fayning notable images of vertues, vices, or what als, with that delightful teaching which must be the right describing note to know a Poet by . . . '[22]

Although Sidney's *Defence* is a reply at least in part to Puritan attack, one must not forget that he was a Puritan himself. He was also a neo-Platonist, a humanist, and certainly a poet.

The seventeenth century provides a literal gold mine for thought on the relation of literary language to spiritual understanding. When John Donne, for example, observes the proliferation of metaphor and figure that pervades God's literal work, he ecstatically exclaims:

> My God, my God, thou art a direct God, may I not say a literal
> God, a God that wouldst be understood literally . . . but thou
> art also . . . a figurative, a metaphorical God too; a God in whose
> words there is such a height of figures, such voyages, such
> peregrinations to fetch remote and precious metaphors . . . such
> curtains of allegories, such third heavens of hyperboles . . .[23]

Without question, John Bunyan saw, at least to some extent, something of this poetic texture in the Bible, the book that he knew best. He believes in the unique power of imaginative literature. What he says of literary theory, though not incisively argued, demonstrates his belief that the Bible contains literary genius and metaphorical language. He further suggests that imaginative literature has the capacity to teach, to give pleasure, to move, and to refer to webs of meaning beyond the literal text.

The rhymed preface of Part One of *The Pilgrim's Progress* suggests both Bunyan's appreciation of and arguments for the figurative and the imaginative. He says that his allegory is written under the 'Similitude of a Dream'. He praises his 'dark and cloudy words' as embodiments of truth with the capacity to 'Make truth to spangle, and its rays to shine.' He says that he speaks 'in Metaphors' and relies on the authority of the Bible for a method practised by the prophets, Christ, and the apostles. He discerns the multi-dimensional power of 'Parables' to generate new meaning by making words suggest more than they ordinarily mean. He recognises that as a writer 'he makes base things usher in Divine', thus acknowledging that imaginative literature is incarnation, giving body to what had previously been unformed.[24]

In the final section of his preface, he demonstrates a remarkable understanding of the nature of imaginative literature — its illusory quality, its nexus of meaning, its tragicomic essence, and its power to evoke response:

> Would'st thou read Riddles and their Explanation,
> Or else be drownded in thy Contemplation?
> Dost thou love picking-meat? or would'st thou see
> A man i' the Clouds, and hear him speak to thee?
> Would'st thou in a moment Laugh and Weep?
> Would'st thou loose thy self, and catch no harm?
> And find thy self again without a charm?
> Would'st read thyself, and read thou know'st not what
> And yet know whether thou art blessed or not,
> By reading the same lines? O then come hither,
> And lay my Book, thy Head and Heart together. (p. 7)

In theory then, Bunyan asserts his confidence in imaginative literature and clearly suggests that it involves invention and the 'making' of something new. That he believes readers should seriously examine his shaped and interpreted experiences is clearly evident in his urgent note in 'The Conclusion' to Part One of *The Pilgrim's Progress*:

> Take heed also that thou be not extream,
> In playing with the out-side of my Dream:
> Nor let my figure, or similitude,
> Put thee into a laughter or a feud;
>
> . . .
>
> Put by the Curtains, look within my Vail;
> Turn up my Metaphors, and do not fail:
> There, if thou seekest them, such things to find,
> As will be helpful to an honest mind. (p. 164)

Without question this urgent advice embraces his strong desire that his imaginative writing be didactic. He frequently avows his didactic intentions whether he is writing his first allegory and suggesting that 'The Fisher Man . . . to catch the Fish . . . ingageth all his Wits' or writing his spiritual autobiography in order that the 'goodness and beauty of God' towards him might be 'the more advanced and magnified' before others. He also declares his didactic intentions, whether arguing theological issues in

Justification by Faith (IV, p. 220),[25] or teaching children basic
tenets of his faith in *Instruction for the Ignorant* or explicating a
passage from Scripture in *Sighs from Hell* (I, p. 133), or constructing
one of his numerous sermons, *Resurrection of the Dead* (I, p. 363). It
is true then that he believes that his writing should reveal truth, but
it is equally true that Bunyan strongly holds that his 'similitudes'
conceal truth. In *Ebal and Gerizim* he refers to 'setting out' truth in
similitudes to be like 'a painting on a wall,' helping one understand what Hell is like (IV, p. 441). Again, he says in *Solomon's
Temple Spiritualized*, 'O! What speaking things are types, shadows
and parables' (III, p. 249), and he states in *The Saint's Knowledge of
Christ's Love* that 'Christ condescends to our capacities' in 'making
use of . . . similitudes' (IV, p. 86 – 7).

If he writes of his desire to teach, so similarly he speaks of his
desire to please. In *Profitable Meditations*, a small volume of verse,
he says, 'Men's heart is apt in Meeter to delight / Also in that to
bear away the more.' In a subsequent stanza, he states, 'When Doctors give their Physick to the Sick / They make it pleasing with
some other thing.'[26] To those who fear his allegorical mode, he
further acknowledges the need to please:

> Come, Truth, although in Swadling-clouts, I find
> Informs the Judgement, rectifies the Mind,
> Pleases the Understanding, makes the Will
> Submit; the Memory too it doth fill
> With what doth our Imagination please;
> Likewise, it tends our troubles to appease. (p. 5)

In the Preface to the second part of *The Pilgrim's Progress*,
Bunyan is so confident that one can teach and please simultaneously that he has little sympathy for one who is less perceptive.
To those who seem incapable or unwilling to comprehend his
work in his dark 'Words and Storys,' he responds:

> I also know, a dark Similitude
> Will on the Fancie more it self intrude,
> And will stick faster in the Heart and Head,
> Then things from Similies not borrowed. (p. 171)

Although containing less poetic theory than the prefaces to
Parts One and Two of *The Pilgrim's Progress*, the Preface to *The*

Holy War repeats his conviction that similitudes point towards 'all sorts of inward rarities,' or again, he shows his belief in the power of figurative language to embody Christian truth. Again, in *The Pilgrim's Progress* he wants one 'to chuse' to be a pilgrim. To those whom he addresses as 'children' in *Grace Abounding*, he says their 'hungerings and thirstings also after further acquaintance with the Father' is 'great refreshment' to him, and he enjoins them to commune with their own heart and to 'leave no corners unsearched' and to remember the Word 'that first laid hold' upon them (pp. 1, 3).[27] And in *Divine Emblems*, he muses on the good preacher who 'doth the heart so reach / that it doth joy or sigh before the Lord' (IV, p. 457). What Bunyan shows is that qualities which he believes to be characteristic of literature enhance the edification and the pleasure of the reader.

Like numerous writers of the era and in the tradition in which he writes, Bunyan thinks of the literary artist not as one who must exclusively impose order upon life, but rather as one who begins with the belief that order is implicit in the universe because an Omnipotent God is in control. What this suggests is that the writer shows the already existing order in such a way that characters, events and images point towards the invisible God behind that order. Furthermore, things and events in the world are emblems or symbols of spiritual matters. A stalk of grain, a flock of birds, a hive of bees, a spider in a web, and whatever one observes, are charged with significant meaning and are analogous to transcendent spiritual truths. From the Book he knows best, Bunyan sees that familiar and commonplace words like pearls, wine skins, seeds, camels and needles, wayward sons, a clay lamp, a city on a hill, a lost sheep, and other ordinary terms become suggestive of reality beyond themselves and embody spiritual truths.

If Bunyan believes in theory that the unique task of the writer is to embody the familiar in a new language, to incarnate the enigmas of existence in concrete terms, and to shape human experience into an imaginative construct, then it is reasonable to expect writings of literary artistry. The extent to which these reasonable expectations are justifiable may be understood from five major imaginative works: *Grace Abounding, The Pilgrim's Progress* (Parts One and Two), *The Life and Death of Mr. Badman, The Holy War,* the *Emblems* and from the sermon treatises. In an attempt to study his works in various genres, my primary concern is not to defend Bunyan's artistry, or lack of it, but rather to call attention to literary qualities that characterise his writing. In turn, these discovered qualities tell on their own merit a more complete story of John Bunyan as an imaginative writer.

Notes

1. The English Association Leaflet, Letter No. 19 (London, 1911), p. 11.

2. Quoted in J.W. Cross, *George Eliot's Life as Related in Her Letters and Journals* (Edinburgh and London, 1885), II, p. 143

3. 'Of Allegory', *Transactions of the Royal Society of Literature of the United Kingdom*, second series, XXVII (London, 1907), p. 48.

4. Clifford Kent Wright, *Bunyan as a Man of Letters* (Oxford, 1916), pp. 11–12.

5. Angus Fletcher, *The Theory of Symbolic Mode* (Ithaca, 1914), p. 346.

6. William Hamilton Nelson, *Tinker and Thinker, John Bunyan, 1628–1688* (New York, 1928), p. 35, somewhat apologetically writes that *The Holy War* had a great deal to commend it even though there are places where it is unnatural, ponderous, and farfetched. Henri Talon, *John Bunyan The Man and His Works* (Cambridge, 1951), p. 139, states that there are passages in *Grace Abounding* which enable us to see the spontaneous genius with which Bunyan dramatises his experiences. Roger Sharrock, *John Bunyan* (London, 1954), p. 117, insists that *The Life and Death of Mr. Badman* is 'too well written to be handed over to the social historian, however much its merits may have been exaggerated by the enthusiasts of realism.'

7. Edward Charles Wagenknecht, *Cavalcade of the English Novel* (New York, 1954), p. 23.

8. James Anthony Froude, *John Bunyan* (New York, 1880), p. 109.

9. William York Tindall, *John Bunyan: Mechanick Preacher* (New York, 1964), p. vii.

10. Émile Legouis, 'The Dissident Writers', *A History of English Literature* (London, 1926), p. 693.

11. Sir Charles Firth, 'John Bunyan', *Essays Historical and Literary* (Oxford, 1938), p. 133.

12. Sharrock, *John Bunyan*, pp. 141–2, 144.

13. Talon, *John Bunyan The Man and His Works*, p. 134.

14. D.W. Robertson Jr., *A Preface to Chaucer* (Princeton, 1960), p. 60.

15. Bernard F. Huppé, 'Introduction', *A Reading of the Canterbury Tales* (Albany, 1967), pp. 5–6.

16. Robertson, *A Preface to Chaucer*, p. 53.

17. *On Christian Doctrine*, translated by D.W. Robertson Jr. (New York, 1958), p. 38.

18. *A Preface to Chaucer*, p. 58.

19. *Boccaccio on Poetry*, edited and translated by C.G. Osgood (New York, 1956), p. 59.

20. For further insight see *A Preface to Chaucer*, particularly pp. 80–3. Bernard F. Huppé, *A Reading of the Canterbury Tales*, also shows the echoing of the Augustinian theory in Chaucer. For a succinct survey of the Augustinian tradition, please see Bernard F. Huppé and D.W. Robertson Jr. *Fruyt and Chaf* (Princeton, 1963), Chap 1.

21. *Apologie for Poetrie*, ed. Edward Arber (Westminster, 1901), p. 28.

22. Ibid., p. 29.

23. John Donne, *Devotions upon Emergent Occasions* (Michigan, 1959), p. 124.

24. 'The Author's Apology for His Book', *The Pilgrim's Progress,* ed. James Blanton Wharey, 2nd edn, Roger Sharrock (London, 1960), pp. 1–6.

25. Except where stated differently, quotations are from *The Entire Works of John Bunyan,* ed. Henry Stebbing, 4 vols. (London, 1862).

26. John Bunyan, *Profitable Meditations, Fitted to Man's Different Condition, In a Conference Between Christ and a Sinner* (London, 1661), p. 4.

27. Quotations are from *Grace Abounding* and *The Pilgrim's Progress,* ed. Roger Sharrock (London, 1966), p. 4.

2 *GRACE ABOUNDING*

Central to the seventeenth century are intense theological concerns.[1] Proponents of various persuasions were expected to search for religious understanding, and to determine to what extent the Scriptures, the traditions of the Church, the Book of Nature, the promptings of the 'inner voice', and the reason of man could be trusted as reliable guides. The resultant findings were not only significant aspects of epistemological debates upon which the philosophers of the age exercised themselves, but for the spiritual man, they were fundamental to his view of self and the relation of that self to a transcendent reality that gave meaning to life's experiences. The belief that the individual could and should scrutinise the state of his spiritual welfare was an assumption shared by both Puritans and non-Puritans.[2] The process and results of such scrutiny moved directly into the written record of numerous authors of the seventeenth century and was the source of one of the most popular literary genres of the period, the spiritual autobiography.

Between 1600 and 1640 autobiographies were written sporadically, three or four each decade. But during the 1640s and 1650s the number doubled and doubled once more during the 1660s, continuing at that level until the close of the century. The number written by Anglicans remained fairly constant, about two or three each decade, but there came a sudden increase after 1640, as Dean Ebner clearly shows, to the increasing individualism of the Puritan movement. Each Puritan sect shared to a greater degree than did the non-Calvinists that distinctive individualism which emphasised the priesthood of all believers, consequently eliminating an intermediary between God and man but at the same time entrusting the individual with primary responsibility for exploring and understanding the nature of his own spiritual needs.[3]

Since there are universal and recurrent elements in the soul's experiences, and since similarities in Christian experience enabled others to measure their own spiritual growth, these factors explain not only a wide writing but a wide reading of spiritual autobiographies in the seventeenth century.[4]

Although there can be a strong relationship between theological doctrine and spiritual autobiography, the two must not be confused. Roy Pascal is accurate in contending that the 'autobiography is not an appropriate means to urge the objective truth of a doctrine — though it may reveal more profound and general truths of life which the doctrine only partially formulates'.[5] What Pascal sees is that autobiography is a literary genre, and it communicates by indirection — the way all literature communicates. Autobiography is, as Sally McFague states, 'a story of a life, and the best autobiographies are written precisely as a story, that is, as an ordering of events around a central focus'.[6] The story should not, however, be confused with memoirs in which an author simply relates *facts* about his childhood, his ancestors, his education, his career, and his beliefs. Nor should the 'story' in autobiography be confused with diaries or journals which depict with a minimal degree of selectivity a series of events and interactions in an individual's life. 'What one seeks in reading autobiography,' says James Olney, 'is not a date, a name, or a place, but a characteristic way of perceiving, or organizing, and of understanding, an individual way of feeling and expressing . . .'[7]

To write then of external circumstances in a life, based exclusively upon verifiable facts, is to write something other than autobiography. As a literary genre, autobiography scrutinises the inner landscape and gives order and meaning to past experiences from a present perspective. The main thrust of autobiography is to show *who* someone *is*. Roy Pascal explains the thrust and major components of autobiography in these words:

> The truly autobiographical impulse is to recapture the past, to see one's life as a whole, to find within its vagaries one rapture and one indivisible personality . . . The life is represented in autobiography not as something established, but as a process; it is not simply the narrative of the voyage, but also the voyage itself. . . This is the decisive achievement of the art of autobiography: to give us events that are symbolic of the personality as an entity unfolding not solely according to its own laws, but also in response to the world it lives in. Through them both the writers and readers know life. It is not necessarily or primarily an intellectual or scientific knowledge, but a knowing

through the imagination, a sudden grasp of reality through reliving it in the imagination, an understanding of the feel of life, the feel of living.[8]

The major features of autobiography are evident in the quoted passage: focusing on a 'self', an 'indivisible personality', the recapturing of a past, the unfolding of incidents as part of one process, the scrutinising of the inner landscape and its harmony with the outer world, and a 'grasping of reality through reliving it in the imagination — or knowing through the literary ways of autobiography. A spiritual autobiography is similar except that the 'self' is examined in its relation to God. John Bunyan's spiritual autobiography is certainly no exception.

Grace Abounding, published in 1666, was written sometime during Bunyan's imprisonment in Bedford Jail from 1600–72, or when he was between the age of 31 to 43. The work focuses on a 'self', one central character, briefly as a child, as a young married man leaning towards the Anglican Church, as one with a growing sensitivity to God and an abhorrence for sin and as one who put on an outward reformation and tried to study the Bible. The self continues to unfold as he ponders the joy of some 'poor women' of Bedford, as he denies his 'carnal friends', as he turns again to a study of the Bible, and as he begins to fear that he may not be among the elect. The inner landscape consists continually of tensions between doubt and despair, joys and sorrow, love and fear, struggle and rest, and finally, with the relaxing of tension, an admiration for the wisdom of God. This pattern corroborates Sallie McFague's words that the 'theologian-autobiographer becomes not the vessel of an idea or belief (a spatial metaphor), but a map of the movements of a belief in a human life (a linear metaphor)'.[9]

To discover how Bunyan constructs 'the map' is a key to understanding his spiritual autobiography as an imaginative work of literature. How does he tell 'his story'? And, with what thoroughness does he mark the 'map of the movement'? A close look at the shape of his imaginative construct is essential in determining a response to these crucial questions.

Critics suggest various approaches to the study of the spiritual autobiography. L.S. Lerner's fixed pattern of five stages for spiritual autobiography has merit: serious childhood, sinful youth, legal righteousness often preceded by a struggle, and final illumination.[10] Margaret Bottrall sees the pattern as 'devotion, propaganda, and catharsis',[11] while Roger Sharrock thinks the conventional divisions of autobiography to be four stages: before conversion, conversion, calling, and ministry.[12] James Thorpe suggests that the most illuminating way to describe Bunyan's autobiography is to observe that it consists of two major parts and a series of short anticlimaxes. The first part (sections 1–139) Thorpe calls 'Before the Fall', the second part (sections 140–252) might be called 'After the Fall', and Thorpe views sections 253–339 as a series of three anticlimaxes. Then follows the formal 'Conclusion', with its seven sections.[13]

Each of the aforementioned suggestions is *one* way of observing the structural development of spiritual autobiography and of *Grace Abounding*, but Thorpe's view in particular fails to sharpen the stage which must have been climactic for Bunyan, not only in his spiritual experience but in the structure of the autobiography. If Bunyan's strong beliefs in original sin and in Christ's atoning grace to release the individual from the power of sin are informing principles of his autobiography, then one has a right to expect the moment of release as a pivotal point in the structure of the literary work. Bunyan shows exactly this!

A helpful way to see the unity of the work is to note the following stages: Stranger to Grace (sections 1–36), Movement towards Grace (sections 37–229), Advent of Grace (section 230), Discoveries in Grace (sections 231–339). The first stage begins with an account of his youthful wickedness and God's manifest care for him, proceeds with his questionings concerning his eligibility for God's grace, and concludes with his decision to 'taste the sweetness' of any sin he had not yet experienced, exploring simultaneously attempts at legal righteousness, though he asserts that during these periods 'he knew not Christ nor grace'.

But the second part, the Movement towards Grace, begins when he hears the conversation of three or four poor women in Bedford who speak of 'a new birth' and the 'work of God in their hearts'. Bewildered by this new language, Bunyan concludes that they speak 'with such appearance of grace' that they appear to him as having found 'a new World'. Their talk of free grace appeals to him and he becomes temporarily encouraged, but questions and doubts begin to overwhelm him: What if the day of grace is passed for him? What if he is not among the elect? These and similar questions divide his soul; he longs for Someone or Something to bring peace and relief to his tormented self: 'But oh, how I now loved these words that spoke of a *Christian's calling*! as when the Lord said to one *Follow me*, and to another, *Come after me*, and oh, thought I, that he would say so to me too! how gladly would I run after him.'[14]

Attacks of despair, a sense of dreadful guilt, and an awareness of inward pollution so plague him that he believes without equivocation that the condition of his soul 'could not stand with a state of grace'. The tension of trying to believe but sinking further into unbelief and despair all but exhausts him. Later, for a while, he is so sure that he had experienced 'a true manifestation of grace' that he thinks he could speak of God's mercy even 'to the very Crows that sat upon the plow'd lands before him'. But within a week or two the scriptural statement, 'Simon, Simon, behold Satan hath desired to have you', haunts him so convincingly that on one occasion he turns his head to determine who calls him. The juxtaposition of hope and despair continue until the temptation to 'sell Christ' presents itself,·and highly dramatic is the 'to sell Christ' episode. In a prologue-like soliloquy, Bunyan discusses the early beginning of the temptation, depicts the stages of its intensity, expresses the agony of the conflict, and develops the entire episode to a tremendous climax with cries, 'Sell him, sell him', mingling with the injunction, 'Let him go, if he will'. Great ingenuity is exercised here; the dramatic action proceeds from 'the inner stage', carried forward through reflection on his condition and expression of emotional turmoil involved, until finally a man who has lost a battle takes shape before him: 'now', says Bunyan, 'was the battel won, and down I fell, as a Bird that is shot from the top of a Tree, into great guilt and fearful despair'.[15]

After a brief respite from his tormented state, Bunyan begins to doubt again and wishes himself anything but a man and in any condition but his own. The monologues and dialogues, showing the dynamic flux of the inner life, continue. He 'strives' with Satan over John's statement, 'him that comes, I will in no wise cast out', he recalls in turbulent distress the story of Esau's selling his birthright, he ponders the possibility of disagreement in Scriptures on the salvation of a soul; but distress becomes interspersed with comfort, potential conflicts in scriptural accounts become erased as he weighs and clarifies, and his movement towards grace becomes complete as he concludes that his 'good frame of heart' made not his 'righteousness better' nor did his 'bad frame' make his 'righteousness worse', for his righteousness was 'Jesus Christ himself'.

The Advent of Grace immediately follows. 'Now did my chains,' says Bunyan, 'fall off my legs indeed' (section 230). This is the climax of the autobiography; he is now 'loosed from his afflictions and irons'. The climax is not later when he speaks of seeing new 'heights and depths in Grace' (section 252), nor is it when he exclaims to his wife, 'O now I know, I know!' (section 263), nor is it during the game at cat, as Vera Brittain states,[16] when he hears a voice curtailing his 'second strike'. The former statements refer to new insights gained by the new believer after temporary periods of temptation and restlessness; the latter are the early hints of a long inner struggle which finally lead to his conversion experience and the assurance of his 'effectual calling'.

Following the Advent of Grace, Bunyan continues his introspective analysis, for never does he leave for any length of time the development of his inner life. He probes the causes of temptation and the resulting advantages to the growth of his soul of endured temptations, one of the primary advantages being his concentrated study of the Scriptures without fear of what he might uncover. No longer is he the victim of a tortured mind; he now discovers with a new perception an enormous abundance of grace and rejoices in God's wisdom.

The major structure of *Grace Abounding* concludes with his attainment of an unparalleled peak of exultation in his vision of the saints passing over into the New Jerusalem. But two separate headings follow, 'A Brief Account of the Imprisonment' and a 'Conclusion', including seven sections. No damage is done to the thematic structure through these loosely constructed sections, for certainly one manifestation of 'grace abounding' is the consciousness of a call to a special vocation, and further manifestation of grace is evident in Bunyan's awareness of God's work in every detail of experience — even in his imprisonment. Intertwined with this evidence of God's grace is a subject to which Bunyan has devoted many pages of the autobiography, the subtlety of the presence and the power of temptation. Not once does he suggest that his new discoveries in grace obviate the fact that other battles await him, for no man is free from temptations and conflicts as long as he lives in temporal time.

Grace Abounding, then, is a graphic picture of the intense spiritual struggle through which Bunyan went. Throughout the long journey there is no indication that he wants simply to glorify the struggle or to magnify the anguish of self-examination; he wants to *know* and he wants his knowledge to have a biblical basis. That he tells his story through the lenses of his own theology is at once clear: man is sinful but yet morally responsible, and free grace is his if he will accept it, and it is the only route man can take in order to know any relief from the consciousness of guilt.

But the aim of spiritual autobiography is literary, not propagandist, and though John Bunyan writes a book to delineate his struggle, he paradoxically writes a work that belongs to a reputable literary genre, the same in which Augustine writes the *Confessions*, the first spiritual autobiography. In referring to the *Confessions*, Sallie McFague says that Augustine is 'the first one to toil in the "heavy soil" of his own memory in order to recollect his own spiritual evolution'.[17] Bunyan also remembers and analyses his past, and in the chronological stages from his being a stranger to Grace, to the advent of Grace, to the discoveries in Grace, no external event or internal struggle is too small for his closest scrutiny. Departing from her usual perceptive insights, Joan Webber suggests that Bunyan's prose lacks the atmosphere of solitude and that the 'I' of his narrative is in constant contact with everyday, outdoor activity and further, not only is he not in prison, he is also never at home.[18] But this seems to disregard several important facts: the Preface, with its Pauline-letter tone, surely suggests his imprisonment when he writes of looking after his 'children' from the lion's den; the agony which he describes in leaving his family, especially his blind child; an understanding, gained in the process of suffering, that sent him 'mourning home'; and the struggles within the inner landscape that pervade the work from the beginning to the end, struggles which are primarily his alone. Far more important, however, than contact with 'everyday, outdoor activity' or whether he is at home or in prison is Bunyan's recollection of the self in relation to God. He begins his recollections with the location of his inner experiences in temporal time. He speaks of the length of time, days, weeks, or months, during which he has endured the tensions of conflict. Or, he recalls that on a particular day he is in a certain state of *mind*; indeed, 'sighs and tears and groans/Show minutes, times, and hours'. Consider these sections:

> Thus I went on for many weeks, sometimes comforted, and sometimes tormented; and, especially at some times, my

torment would be very sore, for all those Scriptures forenam'd in the *Hebrews* would be set before me, as the only sentences that would keep me out of Heaven. Then, again, I should begin to repent, that every thought went THOROW me; I should also think thus why myself, why, How many Scriptures are there against me? there is but three or four, and cannot God miss them, and save me for all of them? Sometimes again I should think, O if it were not for these three or four words, now how might I be comforted! And I could hardly forbear at some times, but to wish them out of the Book. (section 208).

On other occasions, events of a particular day tear him apart:

And I remember one day, as I was in diverse frames of Spirit, and considering that these frames were still according to the nature of the several Scriptures that came in upon my mind; if this of Grace, then I was quiet; but if that of Esau, then tormented. Lord, thought I, if both these Scriptures could meet in my heart at once, I wonder which of them would get the better of me . . . (section 212)

Although his autobiography is a remembrance of time past, Bunyan gives an immediacy to his struggle. As in *The Pilgrim's Progress*, he frequently uses the words 'now' and 'then', not only as connectives, and they certainly do connect, but also to give a sense of the present to his narrative. In three successive sections, he says: 'And now began I to labour to call again time that was past; wishing a thousand times twice told, that the day was yet to come when I should be tempted to such a sin . . .' (section 150). He follows: 'Then again, being loath and unwilling to perish, I began to compare my sin with others, to see if I could find that any of those that are saved had done as I had done . . .' (section 151). As if 'now' and 'then' were in combat, he adds, 'Now again should I be as if racked upon the Wheel; when I considered, that, besides the guilt that possessed me, I should be *so* void of grace, *so* bewitched: What, thought I, must it be no sin but this? . . .' (section 152). This sense of immediacy is further enhanced by speaking in the past tense, only to follow through with the use of the present: 'Methought the Judge stood at the door, I was as if 'twas come already: so that such things could have no entertainment; but methinks I see by this that Satan will use any means to keep the Soul from Christ . . .' (section 162).

The immediacy as well as the constancy of the struggle is further re-enforced by the way in which he stacks up participles. One illustration will suffice:

> Once as I was walking to and fro in a good mans Shop, bemoaning to myself in my sad and doleful state, afflicting myself with self abhorrence for this wicked and ungodly thought; lamenting also this hard hap of mine . . . greatly fearing I should not be pardoned; praying also in my heart . . . and being now ready to sink with fear . . . (section 174)

In his movement towards Grace, Bunyan finds much of life only a sequence of conflicts and uncertainties, strung together in a time-succession. Pressing upon his thinking is belief in a certainty and an immortality not known in terms of time. Hence much of his musing wavers between the actualities of temporal time and the realities that are transtemporal. At that climactic moment when he knows the advent of Grace and has just exclaimed that he is loosed from his 'afflictions and irons', there is still evidence of this momentary and transient wavering:

> . . . so that from that time those dreadful Scriptures of God left off to trouble me; now went I also home rejoycing, for the grace and love of God: So when I came home, I looked to see if I could find that Sentence, *Thy Righteousness is in Heaven*, but could not find such a Saying, wherefore my Heart began to sink again, onely that was brought to my remembrance, *He of God is made unto us Wisdom, Righteousness, Sanctification, and Redemption* . . . (section 230)

If he brings his intense struggle to the present and if his spirit frequently wavers between the pressures of temporal time and the realities of the transtemporal, Bunyan also remembers that his is a world that has meaning because an omniscient God rules over it and no one internal struggle or external confrontation occurs without significance. Furthermore, each detail is in some particular manner an evidence of God's grace; this characteristic stance is probably no more vividly declared than in these words:

> Now I was, that as God has his hand in all providences and

dispensations that overtook his Elect, so he had his hand in all the temptations that they had to sin against him, not to animate them unto wickedness, but to chuse their temptations and troubles for them; and also to leave them, for a time, to such sins only as might not destroy, but humble them . . . but lay them in the way of renewing of his mercies . . . (section 157)

As if he were attempting to bind together the various aspects of his doubts and conflicts, he gives a crowning statement that summarises the relationship between his experiences and God's grace:

I never saw those heights and depths in grace, and love, and mercy, as I saw after this temptation:[19] great sins do draw out great grace; and where guilt is most terrible and fierce, then the mercy of God in Christ, when showed to the Soul, appears most high and mighty. (section 252)

A vivid imagination is at work in Bunyan's description of his moments of peace or his periods of terror. What the discovery of an old book means to him in his groping moments is dramatically told. Plagued by numerous questions concerning his relationship to Christ, he longs to see some 'ancient Godly man's Experience', who had written hundreds of years before he was born and who had wrestled with questions similar to his. One day he discovers a translation of Luther's *Commentary on Galatians,* and concerning this, Bunyan writes:

Well, after many such longings in my mind, the God in whose hands are all our days and ways, did cast into my hand, one day, a book of *Martin Luther*, his comment on the *Galatians*, so old that it was ready to fall piece from piece, if I did but turn it over. Now I was pleased much that such an old book had fallen into my hand; the which, when I had but a little way perused, I found my condition in his experience, so largely and profoundly handled, as if his book had been written out of my heart; this made me marvel . . . (section 129)

Bunyan further declares that next to the Bible he prefers Luther's commentary above all the books he had ever seen 'as most fit for a wounded conscience'. And passages from this book helped to heal his wounds on numerous occasions when he was torn by doubts and fears.

If Bunyan evidences his vivid imagination in depicting moments of peace and comfort, so similarly does he manifest it in delineating the horrors of his tormented mind and spirit. He becomes subject to such horrible 'thick, coming fancies' that he believes he has either lost his sanity or the devil possesses him. See the agony he unfolds when he describes his tendency to blaspheme God:

> I often, when these temptations have been with force upon me, did compare my self in the case of such a Child, whom some Gypsie hath by force took up under her apron, and is carrying from Friend and Country; kick sometimes I did, and also scream and cry; but yet I was as bound in the wings of the temptation, and the wind would carry me away. (section 102)

Not one of Bunyan's senses escapes the impact of the tension of conflict. In his yearning for peace with God, he reaches a state of discouragement that 'laid him as low as hell' and he declares that even if he should have to burn at a stake he would fail to believe that Christ loves him. In desperation he cries out: 'Alas, I could neither hear him, nor see him, nor feel him, nor savour any of his things. I was driven as with a Tempest.' (section 78).

To re-enforce the agony of torturous struggles upon the movement of his mind, Bunyan often uses numbers to emphasise the severity of the conflict: ' . . . for my peace would be in and out, sometimes twenty times a day' (section 205), or ' . . . why, How many scriptures are there against me? There is but three or four . . . O, if it were not for these three or four words, now how might I be comforted!' (section 208). That haunting temptation 'to sell Christ', too, he says would run in his thoughts 'not so little as a hundred times together'. He knows and does not know, and his less than tranquil recollections perhaps remind the modern reader of the Chorus in *Murder in the Cathedral* when it senses Thomas's 'failure of faith', 'God is leaving us, God is leaving us, more pang, more pain, than birth or death. Sweet and cloying through the dark air / Falls the stifling scent of despair . . .'[20]

Bunyan further sharpens the intensity of the agony by using physical imagery, thus demonstrating that both body and mind are in torture. Numerous episodes declare this meshing of body and mind: '. . . my torment would flame out and afflict me; yea it would grind me as it were to Powder' (section 155). And when he tells of his meeting with that miserable mortal, Francis Spira, he speaks of it as 'a book that was to my troubled spirit as salt when rubbed into a fresh wound' (section 163). Further stressing the intertwining of body and mind, Bunyan cries out in realistic phrasing, 'Then was I struck into a very great trembling, insomuch that at sometimes I could, for whole days together, feel my very body, as well as my minde, to shake and totter . . . I felt also such a clogging and heat at my stomach, by reason of this my terrour, that I was, especially at some times, as if my breastbone would split in sunder . . . ' (section 164). Even in a moment of relief from his torture, the imagery compels the reader to remember his agony. He writes of the quieting impact of a verse of scripture in contrast to his uncertainty and fear: 'This made a strange seisure upon my spirit; it brought light with it, and commanded a silence in my heart of all those tumultuous thoughts that before did use, like masterless hellhounds, to roar and bellow, and make a hideous noise within me' (section 174). What Charles W. Baird says of other incidents of the forces of physical impact is appropriate: 'The dominant tone is that of objective drama, rather than of either subjective didacticism or sentimental indulgence, because the movement of mind is recreated directly and the conflicts of ideas are "rendered" dramatically.'[21]

Bunyan's imagery frequently suggests destruction, especially in his references to animals and weapons. Not only are there the 'masterless hellhounds', but he also writes of the Lamb, the Saviour, turning 'lion and destroyer'; furthermore, he states that the story of Esau's selling his birthright stands 'like a spear' against him, and he also often feels as if God conceals Himself 'with a flaming sword'.

At times he uses verbs to show the degree and extent of his deplorable condition: doubts and questions would *confound* him, *imprison* him, *vex* him, and *tie* him up from faith. There is a simplicity about his imagery, but it is powerful in its unveiling of the tormented intensity of Bunyan's mind and spirit in his movement towards the grace of God.

Bunyan also fills his autobiography with rich similes,[22] in fact, this is perhaps his most pervasive figure of speech. He orders these to show the tumult of struggle, the sense of bondage, the longing for release. When he compares his own sin with that of Judas, he bemoans that he is 'tossed to and fro like the Locusts, and driven from trouble to sorrow . . . ' (section 158). Or, when he reflects on the words which tell of Esau's inability to find a place of repentance, he says, 'These words were to my soul like fetters of brass to my legs' (section 143).

Concrete language also augments the intensity and strain of Bunyan's struggle: 'The glory of the Holiness of God did at this time break me to pieces, and the Bowels and Compassion of Christ did break me as on the Wheel' (section 244); 'Now was my soul greatly pinched between these two considerations: live I must not, Die I dare not' (section 257); ' . . . then, with great force hath the Tempter laboured to distract me and confound me and to turn away my mind . . . ' (section 108).

Concreteness is, of course, an aspect of the plain style in which Bunyan deliberately chooses to write. Before concluding his prefatory note, he states that he wants to be plain and simple even though he could have 'stepped into a stile much higher' and 'could have adorned all things more'. William O. Haller aptly reminds us that the boast of plainness among the Puritan preachers should not be taken literally, for a plain style is neither colourless and prosaic nor unimaginative and unliterary but rather it is a style designed to be intelligible.[23] Details of seventeenth-century contentions over stylistic theories and practices have been traced in many scholarly articles and books,[24] but, Bunyan, ill-equipped to enter into the scholarly controversies over style, still has his own convictions about not using an 'adorned' style:

> *but I dare not: God did not play in convincing of me; the Devil did not play in tempting of me; neither did I play when I sunk as into a bottomless pit, when the pangs of hell caught hold upon me: wherefore I may not play in my relating of them: but be plain and simple, and lay down the thing as it was . . .*[25]

But in his desire not 'to play' but rather to be 'plain and simple', he is still able to create laudatory imaginative effects in the style which he chooses.

To heighten the rhythm he uses reiteration, italicisation and direct quotation, the latter usually coming from the Bible; at times, too, even in one section he moves from the intensely lyrical to what modern critics might call a stream of consciousness:[26]

Once I was much troubled to see whether the Lord Jesus was both Man as well as God, and God as well as Man; and truly in those dayes, let men say what they would, unless I had it with evidence from Heaven, all was as nothing to me, I counted not myself set down in any truth of God; well, I was much troubled about this point, and could not tell how to be resolved: at last, that in the fifth of the *Revelations* came into my mind, *And I beheld, and lo, in the midst of the Throne and of the four Beasts and in the midst of the Elders stood a Lamb;* In the midst of the Throne, thought I, there is his Godhead, in the midst of the Elders, there is his man hood; but O methought this did glister, it was a goodly touch and gave me sweet satisfaction . . . (section 122)

Equally compelling is his dialectic precision. One illustration of the way this pulls a reader into Bunyan's own self-exploration will suffice:

. . . then the Tempter again laid at me very sore, suggesting, That neither the mercy of God, nor yet the blood of Christ, did at all concern me, nor could they help me, for my sin; therefore it was but in vain to pray. Yet, thought I, I will pray. But, said the Tempter, your sin is unpardonable. Well, said I, I will pray. 'Tis no boot said he. Yet, said I, I will pray. So I went to prayer to God; and while I was at prayer, I uttered words to this effect: *Lord, Satan tells me, That thy Mercy, nor Christs blood is sufficient to save my soul: Lord, shall I honour thee most by believing thou wilt and canst, or him, by believing thou neither wilt nor canst? Lord, I would fain honour thee by believing thou wilt and canst.* (section 200)

Brief reference should be made to another characteristic of Bunyan's literary art, the small allegory, which foreshadows the method he would use with enormous success in *The Pilgrim's Progress.* One of the most effective examples is the one concerning the poor women of Bedford whom he overhears talking about a 'new birth, the work of God on their hearts'. After leaving them, he later sees them 'in a kind of Vision'; they seem 'as if they were set on the Sunny side of some high Mountain'. He sees also a wall surrounding this mountain that appears to exclude him from the sunshine of God's mercy. After searching again and again around that wall, Bunyan finds a narrow passage, not unlike the Wicket Gate which

Christian later would find, through which he could enter if he would forsake the world and sin, for here was 'roome for Body and Soul' but not for 'Body and Soul, and Sin'. With a slight touch Bunyan conveys the entire scene of the women in discussion of the new birth, and through the tendency toward allegory, gives broader ramifications to his individual experience.

Desiring to express his own urgent need and to teach others by a straightforward account of his conflicts, Bunyan writes a spiritual autobiography of considerable literary merit. His mind, filled with topics and concerns gathered first hand from observation, suffering, and reflection, sorts out what is most urgent, reviews his life from a particular perspective, and gives meaning to past experiences from his present vantage point.

Unafraid to be personal, Bunyan focuses on both the sequence of the struggle and clarification of its stages; from his perspective he selects, structures, and interprets the varied features of the tumultuous route from his state of alienation from Grace to his assurance of 'grace abounding' in his personal life. Throughout the entire way, the reader recognises, as stated earlier, a characteristic way of perceiving, of understanding, of feeling, and of expressing. He is also a witness to the unfolding of a personality. The route Bunyan assesses is the direction *his* life takes and no doubt in its broad outlines is the order which he would prescribe for all individuals of all times. Obviously, there are those who have little sympathy for Bunyan's 'map', but it is indisputable that so long as the large questions of human experience vex the thinking individual of any era who is trying to know himself and the One beyond himself, then so long will Bunyan's *Grace Abounding*, through its own literary ways, make its appeal to the searching mind.[27]

Years passed before Bunyan made his struggles the groundwork of a story presenting not only his experience, but also the general experience of everyman who quests for righteousness and meaning. In the meantime the training he went through tended to fit him for the task towards which *Grace Abounding* already hints: the writing of allegory. Assiduous reading of the Bible and of the few religious books he possessed had been to him a new education; diligent preaching, exact searching, controversial writing, and keen observing completed the process.

Notes

1. See Helen C. White, *English Devotional Literature (Prose), 1600–1640* (Madison, 1931). Note especially pp. 10–30.

2. William Haller, *The Rise of Puritanism* (New York, 1938), writes in Chapter 3 on the scrutiny of the soul as a distinctively Puritan experience. See also Charles H. and Catherine George, *The Protestant Mind of the English Reformation (1570–1640)* (Princeton, 1961), pp. 298ff., for an excellent discussion of the view that conviction, following scrutiny of the soul, is typical of the Protestant outlook.

3. Dean Ebner, *Autobiography in Seventeenth Century England* (The Hague, 1971), p. 17.

4. G.A. Starr, *Defoe and Spiritual Autobiography* (Princeton, 1965), pp. 17–18.

5. Roy Pascal, *Design and Truth in Autobiography* (Cambridge, Mass., 1960), p. 182.

6. Sallie McFague, *Speaking in Parables* (Philadelphia, 1975), p. 145.

7. James Olney, *Metaphors of Self: The Meaning of Autobiography* (Princeton, 1972), p. 37.

8. Pascal, *Design and Truth in Autobiography*, pp. 24, 182, 185.

9. McFague, *Speaking in Parables*, pp. 157–8.

10. *Hibbert Journal*, LV (July, 1957), pp. 373–4.

11. Margaret Bottrall, *Every Man a Phoenix* (London, 1958), p. 84.

12. Roger Sharrock, ed. *Grace Abounding* (Oxford, 1962), p. xxx.

13. James Thorpe, ed. *The Pilgrim's Progress and Grace Abounding* (New York, 1969), pp. viii–x.

14. All quotations are from Roger Sharrock, ed. *Grace Abounding and The Pilgrim's Progress* (London, 1966).

15. See sections 135–40 for the dramatic 'Sell Christ' episode.

16. Vera Brittain, *In the Steps of John Bunyan* (New York, 1950), p. 129.

17. McFague, *Speaking in Parables*, p. 162.

18. Joan Webber, *The Eloquent 'I'* (Madison, 1968), p. 26.

19. The temptation to which Bunyan refers is his struggle to believe the words of John 6:37, 'And him that comes to me, I will in no wise cast out.'

20 T.S. Eliot, *Murder in the Cathedral* (New York, 1963), p. 44.

21. Charles W. Baird, *John Bunyan. A Study in Narrative Technique* (Port Washington, New York, 1977), pp. 62–3.

22. Joan Webber says in *The Eloquent 'I'*:

> Simile is a simple way of controlling the imagination, and it is analogous here to the habit of breaking apart generalization and concrete detail, of substituting allegory and personal narrative for symbolism. If you say that one thing is like another, you can keep the two distinct and unconfused in your mind more easily than if you fuse them into metaphor. The one place where Bunyan does not typically use simile is where he literally describes the power that thoughts and words are able to exert upon the mind — 'This thought would when I stood and looked on, continually so shake my mind', or 'these words broke in upon my mind.' p. 45

23. Haller, *The Rise of Puritanism*, pp. 132–3.

24. See George Williamson, *The Senecan Amble* (London, 1951) for a perceptive study of style and for citation of pertinent scholarly studies and viewpoints, including that of the distinguished Morris Croll.

25. 'A Preface' to *Grace Abounding*, pp. 5–6.

26. James Thorpe states that this method (the stream of consciousness), 'which we may think of as modern is in fact one of Bunyan's chief methods for exploring his inner self . . ." (p. xii).

27. In my work on *Grace Abounding* as a spiritual autobiography, I am not unaware of the splendid insights of Rebecca S. Beal in 'Grace Abounding to the Chief of Sinners: John Bunyan's Pauline Epistle', SEL 21 (1981) 148–60. The concept of 'intrinsic genre', which she derives from E.D. Hirsch's work, *Validity in Interpretation* (1967; reprint New Haven: Yale University Press, 1976), becomes for her a critical approach to *Grace Abounding* which explains the meaning of the work in its entirety. Her findings throw light on the work, but in my judgement, her approach complements rather than counters an autobiographical entry into *Grace Abounding*.

3 THE PILGRIM'S PROGRESS

Allegory has a long and reputable history. John Stevens says that it is 'perhaps coterminous with conscious mental experience',[1] and C.S. Lewis contends that allegory, in some sense, belongs 'not to medieval man but to men or even to mind in general'.[2] Both opinions suggest that it is the nature of thought and language to represent what is immaterial in 'picturable' terms.

Despite its history as a reputable literary form, critics continue to sense the need to clarify the nature of allegory. Richard Blackmur calls allegory 'the highest form of the putative imagination' and believes that 'successful allegory', like *Vita Nuova* and *Pilgrim's Progress*, 'requires the preliminary possession of a complete and stable body of belief appropriate to the theme in hand'.[3] The suggested requirement is not restricted, however, to allegory; the same may be said of other symbolic modes.

Isabel MacCaffrey re-enforces Blackmur's statement when she writes: 'if symbols do not directly mirror "reality"; they must at least refer to it obliquely'.[4] She is also judicious in seeking to lay to rest the controversy over symbolism and allegory in arguing that 'allegory and symbolism are two ways of dealing with the "fact" of a genuine congruence between visible and invisible reality, and that they are not mutually exclusive'.[5] This congruence should not be taken, however, as a one to one correspondence but rather as the characteristic substance of either allegory or symbolism; in brief, allegory may contain symbolism and symbolic action may be allegorised.

Edwin Honig perceptively argues that literary allegory cannot be dismissed as mere stuffing to fill out a preconceived theory that opposes a realistic view of life. On the contrary, allegory, which is symbolic in method, is realistic in aim and in the content of its perception. He sees allegory as moving progressively backward, forward, and upward on a three-dimensional continuum.[6] To Honig, then, the progression of an allegory is spiral — virtually simultaneous in all three directions: 'backward to the thing represented (the story, the literal depiction of reality) which is itself symbolic, pregnant with signification, and forward and upward to the consummation of its meaning in the whole work'.[7]

Northrop Frye holds that allegory exists on a continuum ranging from the most explicitly allegorical on one end to the most elusive, anti-explicit at the other. At one end theme is dominant; at the other theme and story are dominant. One part of the spectrum would include works in which details show in somewhat explicit fashion a corresponding set of concepts or meanings; another point of the spectrum would include literature that combines theme and image in varying degrees.[8]

What these scholars suggest is that allegory consists not of rigid, layered series of meanings, and certainly not fixed one-to-one correspondences, but rather it is an imaginative literary genre which may contain several continuing meanings, though not necessarily uninterruptedly.

Allegory may be perceived then as the embodiment of beliefs in concrete form. It is a work in which the author imitates external actualities and at the same time suggests the significance of such imitations by extending a central metaphor and by showing additional analogies. The genre exploits the potentialities of central metaphors, and of subordinate ones, in order to unfold truth effectively and to introduce purposeful elusiveness.

Like other literary genres, allegory reveals the 'rules' by which it is to be read and understood. Because of the open-ended nature of the genre, allegorists offer guidelines in a specially designed manner for reading their works. Dante expresses in the letter believed to have been written to Can Grande his directions for reading and interpreting the *Commedia*.[9] Spenser writes an explanatory letter in preface to *The Faerie Queene*. Boccaccio discloses fuller understanding of his *Eclogues* in a letter to Fra Martino da Signa.[10]

John Bunyan also resorts to extratextual material in guiding the reader through his allegory, *The Pilgrim's Progress*. He is aware of the veil of allegory, and if his guidelines show the reader how to 'look within the veil', they arise out of his theory of poetic or literary truth,[11] for urging one to 'turn up metaphors' or 'to look within the veil' necessitates his having given some thought to a view of art.

In the Rhymed Preface to *The Pilgrim's Progress*, Bunyan unequivocally affirms didacticism as a function of the special kind of response that he wishes his allegory to exact from its readers. He summons the authenticity of Scripture and the authority of Biblical 'types' and 'shadows', parables and metaphors as literary ways of effectively depicting truth. When he speaks of 'feigning', he knows that he must invent a story and give attention to narrative pattern. His purpose is to 'chalk out' the journey of one who seeks 'the everlasting prize'; in brief, the journey is his chief metaphor, and the pervading presence of this allegorical metaphor offers the primary route to the unstated meanings it makes visible. Furthermore, the power of allegory to fill the memory permits Bunyan to break out of temporal into transtemporal time, from which the past and future are seen to form different parts of man's experience as journeyer.[12] He is also aware of the capacity of allegory to train the mind, inform the judgement, to aid the memory, and to please the understanding, a view similar to Peacham, who lists among the purposes of allegory the pleasure it gives the reader's judgement as well as the lively images it imprints on the memory.[13] When he questions whether the reader wishes to be in a dream and yet not sleep,[14] he knows too that his story will eventuate into a dream vision, and that vision will unfold truth.

In pressing for an understanding of the power of his chosen mode to his critics, real or imagined, he appears eager to bypass the disenchantment with allegory which some Puritan believers held, or which Tyndale expressed, 'there is not a more handsome or apt thyng withall, than an allegory, nor a more subtle and pestilente thyng in the world to perswade to false matter'.[15] For Bunyan there exists no justification for such disenchantment; he defends his form by pointing to the substance it contains, as in the comparison of his work with a cabinet enclosing gold, but he does not thereby imply that the form is insignificant. His allegory focuses and shapes new experiences for those readers, who may indeed wonder about the 'truth' of his allegory, and at the same time, aids in fulfilling the need to live more deeply and fully and with greater awareness. Instead of beguiling, his form offers a means for stepping up the intensity of a reader's experience as well as a mirror for clarifying it. Bunyan's numerous protests in attempting to justify his 'similitude' reveal his concern that his work be read as literature, as allegory, and not as doctrinal statements, even though no one can question his firm belief in doctrine. It is quite obvious, as U. Milo Kaufmann suggests, that Bunyan was in truth uncomfortable with the Puritan habit of reducing Biblical metaphor to doctrine.[16]

Essentially, Bunyan thinks of allegory as a persuasive way of making important matters known through figurative expression. Admittedly, it is difficult to show in detail his precise view of the allegorical mode. In different works he uses 'similitude' to refer to types, figures, analogies, metaphors, similes, parables, and on the title page to *The Pilgrim's Progress,* he refers to the similitude of a dream. Although difficulties prevail in terminology, it appears evident that Bunyan used the word 'allegory' to refer to a word setting forth one thing by another primarily through an extended central metaphor. There are, of course, additional literary devices within the allegory. For Bunyan the advantages of his selected mode are both to reveal and to conceal the truth. Through his figurative language, which challenges the reader to deeper exploration through various interpretations of the literal, he also suggests the flexibility of the allegorical mode. This flexibility arises, not from 'layered, one to one' meanings of the literal text, but rather from the narrative which contains several continuing meanings, all of which are not equally present at the same time. When Northrop Frye speaks of the contrapuntal technique of allegory,[17] he suggests something significant about the nature, including the flexibility, of the genre. At times one theme is prominent while others are submerged only to re-emerge and to fuse with the prominent theme. The reading of allegory, then, demands a clear focus on the literal level combined with a willingness to perceive how and when other levels emerge. Careful reading also demands the recognition that 'allegory refers "upward" to the final truths of God, as well as outward to the multiple truths of human life in the middest and forward to figuratively anticipated futures'.[18] As Frye further cautions, allegory is still a structure of images, not of disguised ideas, and commentary has to proceed with it exactly as it does with all other literature, trying to see what precepts and examples are suggested by the imagery as a whole.[19]

Bunyan, then, speaks no less truly for speaking metaphorically or for making literal statements that embody other meanings. Through the central metaphor of the journey, he shows unmistakably the stages of a pilgrimage, filled both with struggles and triumphs of his pilgrim 'in the way' from the City of Destruction to his glorious reception into the Celestial City. Each stage becomes credible to one who recognises that Bunyan places Biblical imperatives and an authentic body of belief as underpinnings of each experience or pattern of experiences which moves teleologically towards an end of history. When Pilgrim becomes alarmingly aware that he is in the City of Destruction, he cries out from a sense of urgent need, a cry impelled by the Biblical 'law', 'Now is the accepted time, behold now is the day of salvation' (II Cor. 6:3). To one who lacks Pilgrim's sense of urgency, as well as his desire to believe the Biblical declaration, his desire to go on a strange journey is utterly incomprehensible. In their mocks and threats the neighbours obviously have no understanding of Pilgrim's sense of need. Obstinate places him among 'the craze-headed coxcombs' who are wise in their own eyes, when he learns that Christian (the name Bunyan later gives him) will 'leave all the world' in order to 'seek an inheritance incorruptible'. Christian's closest relatives are incapable of believing anything to be wrong with their world and blandly diagnose his urgent state as some 'frenzy distemper' that 'got into his head'.

Bunyan, then, begins a narrative in which the central character flees from his own family and neighbours. Christian's metaphorical journey will take him into numerous conflicts with the world, and yet he will go beyond and ultimately out of the world. Behind the story of the entire journey is the 'riddling' nature of Biblical truth; it is this paradoxical law of spiritual truth which not only impels him to begin the journey but propels him on his way from the City of Destruction to the Celestial City.

The course of the journey includes growth in spiritual knowledge in places like the Interpreter's House and the House Beautiful and in conversation with fellow Christians like Faithful and Hopeful. It also entails severe conflicts in the Valley of Humiliation and the Valley of the Shadow of Death, persecution in Vanity Fair, suffering in Doubting Castle, encounters with Ignorance, By-Ends, Little-Faith, flatterers, and the appeals of the By-Path Meadow and the Enchanted Ground. The final obstacle is, of course, the River of Death. There is perhaps no major significance to the order of the various conflicts, but the sequence is of interest. The violent conflicts come early in the pilgrimage, the most fierce and intense being the battle with Apollyon. After facing the possibility of death in his violent encounter with Apollyon, it is by no means illogical that the journey into the Valley of the Shadow of Death is a transition from the Valley of Humiliation. The assaults in Vanity Fair are still violent, but present here is an element of contempt for 'fools', 'Bedlams', and 'outlandish men', whose interest lies not in buying the wares of Vanity Fair but only in buying the truth.

The Doubting Castle experience clearly demonstrates that a pilgrim may go through battles and trials with triumph, only to confront a new hurdle with which he can hardly cope. Neither the constant fighting as in the Apollyon episode nor the continued walking as in the Valley of the Shadow seems adequate in Doubting Castle. What troubles the pilgrim is his inability to win victory over the enemy or to get his key from him; his despair blinds him to the key of the Scriptures, the solution for his previous battles.

Almost at the end of his journey, the pilgrim meets with Little-Faith, implying that although almost every conceivable conflict can be won, there is still the possibility of losing one's way. Equally, there is the possibility of deceit, as in the encounter with Flatterer, and of false appearances as in By-Path Meadow or the Enchanted Ground.

To make the long and arduous journey does not mean that the pilgrim is free from the taunts of the false pilgrim, who is not only ignorant of the right way but deliberately and persistently chooses his own self-designed route. It is possible too to come to the end and to forget, briefly, the 'sweet refreshments' of the past, to ignore, temporarily, the assurance of a future in a 'Land that flows with Milk and Honey', and to face, despairingly, the River of Death which offers 'no bridge to go over'.

But the journey does not stop at the River of Death, neither does Bunyan only depict the conflicts. In the structure of the allegory there is a skilful balance between action and contemplation. This is at once evident in the marvelous balance between the trying obstacles and the various stages of Christian instruction, fellowship, understanding, and joy, which show a progressive growth in the pilgrim — from Evangelist's counsel, in the House Beautiful, in the Interpreter's House, on the Delectable Mountains, and in Beulah. At Beulah the gate of the New Jerusalem is 'within sight', and Christian now rejoices in the delights of his present place: air, sweet and pleasant, birds, continually singing, flowers, appearing in the earth, the sun, shining night and day, and the 'shining Ones', talking to faithful pilgrims, for Beulah is upon the 'Borders of Heaven'. The beauty of the landscape now corresponds to the marked beauty and order of the pilgrim's life; indeed the correlation between the natural and supernatural or the spiritual and geographical comes as a result of the projection of the inward transformation upon the external state of terrain and climate.

Yet in the New Jerusalem, Christian and Hopeful enter a state of rest and happiness that surpasses the sights from the Delectable Mountains and in Beulah and reduces the significance of the numerous hurdles. The two pilgrims, 'transfigured' by their new heavenly garments are with God in the Celestial City, a place of unparalleled beauty and glory. Bunyan's rendering of the journey carefully and imaginatively shows both the battles and the triumphs that constitute the various landmarks in the walk of a pilgrim from the City of Destruction to the City of Heaven.

Bunyan sets the journey of his pilgrim within the matrix of a dream. The narrator walks through 'the wilderness of this world', lights on a 'certain place', and 'dreams a dream'. Bunyan lifts his dream immediately to the metaphorical level when he writes of the world as a wilderness through which the believer travels and begins to show what it means to follow 'in the steps of our father Abraham'.[20] Throughout *The Pilgrim's Progress*, the dream sustains the impression that the narrative is all dreamlike, but it also fixes the symbolic character of the quest and thus discloses the hero's relationship to the goal. Almost immediately *The Pilgrim's Progress* takes on meanings which are reflexive; perhaps most important is that the dream is in a sense truer than reality because it has transforming power, an ordering which leads to a new understanding. What is particularly significant to see is that the dream is part of the unbounded world of the shaping imagination.

Whether we interpret the dream as the work of that inner sense, phantasy, 'which is free during sleep to form varied and strange pictures of "divers kind" — natural, divine, demonical — in the mind',[21] or as a fulfulment of a wish,[22] or as an inexplicable insight from a 'source transcending us',[23] in which the Jungean collective unconscious is central, or as 'a meaningful and significant expression of any kind of mental activity under the condition of sleep',[24] we are aware of particular characteristics common to dreams. We dream in images and these images may be either universal or private, or both; we can distinguish the coherence of the image and its imaginative interpretation. We can experience dreams coming full circle as Vision, and consequently know an immediate conscious apprehension of an invisible world. We can, as Freud suggests, condense multiple aspects of dream-activity into one image, or we can split a single character into several who are exhibited in the narrative as separate figures. Dreams occur in a timeless world, but in terms of a succession of events which do not demand a causal, logical relation.[25]

Bunyan begins the dream with an undefined, unlocalised setting; the narrator lights on a 'certain place' and dreams. In that dream he sees:

> *A Man clothed with Raggs, standing in a certain place, with his face from his own House, a Book in his hand, and a great burden upon his Back.* I looked, and saw him open the Book, and Read therein; and as he read, he wept and trembled, and not being able longer to contain, he brake out with a lamentable cry, saying, what shall I do? (p. 8)

Although Bunyan has obviously used the dream framework to initiate the journey, his placement of concrete detail in this illusory world also seems especially significant: *a man* is introduced, clothed with *rags*, a *burden* on his back, and he asks a specific question. Who the man is and what the significance of the various images is, we do not yet know, but these details are undoubtedly important since Bunyan has enjoined the reader not to stop 'with the outside' of the dream but to 'put by the curtains' and 'turn up the metaphors'.

After he initiates the journey through the dream framework, Bunyan appears most unwilling to permit the reader to forget that he is dreaming, for at least 60 times in Part One, Bunyan uses such expressions as 'now I saw in my dream' or 'then I saw in my dream'. Obviously, Bunyan wishes the reader to heed his earlier injunction, 'Wouldst thou be in a dream and yet not sleep?'; he wants us to stretch out into his timeless world and dream too. In speaking of the allegorical quality of his work, he uses, as stated earlier, such terms as parable, metaphor, shadow, but he continues to fall back on the word dream. By reminding us periodically that this is a dream, Bunyan gives a convincing realism to his vague, illusory world. At the same time, the 'now' and the 'then' fuse the past and the present in the progress of Christian and thus form a credible statement of the growth of a soul from a state of gracelessness to a position of blessedness.

Since the metaphor of sight is the focus of numerous scenes throughout the dream, it should come as no surprise that the narrator frequently declares 'now I saw in my dream' or 'then I saw in my dream'. Indeed, the metaphor of sight could well provide a unifying metaphor for the entire dream vision. What Bunyan does early in his book is to establish two levels of seeing: the visible and the invisible. To see only on the level of the visible is to miss the reasons why a true pilgrim makes the journey. That some of the characters in the allegory see only on the level of the visible clearly shows to what extent they lack the qualities necessary to travel the arduous journey which Christian takes.

Christian's first conversation with Evangelist begins to establish the two levels of *seeing*:

> Then said *Evangelist*, pointing with his finger over a very wide field, Do you see yonder *Wicket gate*? The man said, No. Then said the other, Do you see yonder shining light? He said, I think I do. Then said *Evangelist*, Keep that light in your eyes, and go up directly thereto, so shalt thou see the Gate; at which when thou knowest, it shall be told thee what thou shalt do.
>
> So I saw in my Dream, that the Man began to run; Now he had not run far from his own door, but his Wife and Children perceiving it, began to cry after him to return; but the Man put his fingers in his Ears, and ran on crying, Life, Life, Eternal Life: so he looked not behind him, but fled towards the middle of the Plain. (p. 10)

In this emblematic scene the metaphor of sight pervades. Evangelist sees 'yonder Wicket-gate', but the beginning pilgrim emphatically does not see it. When Evangelist then speaks of 'yonder shining light', the pilgrim falteringly says he thinks he *sees* it, and is told he will *see* the Gate if he keeps that light, which Evangelist apparently sees, in his eye. The narrator sees a man beginning to run; the wife and children perceive or *see* a husband and father literally running from them. That the pilgrim is beginning to see — or at least desires to see — from a vantage point not clear on the visible level, is evident in his cry. 'Life, Life, Eternal Life' and in his refusal to look behind him.

To see only on the visible level is a temptation which thwarts Christian early in his pilgrimage. Convinced by Mr Worldly-Wiseman that he must find Legality, Christian asks the way of him:

Chr.   Sir which is my way to this honest man's house?
Worl.   Do you see yonder high hill?

Chr. Yes, very well.

Worl. By that Hill you must go, and the first house you come to is his.

The faltering pilgrim, who has just said that he thought he saw 'yonder shining light', is now absolutely sure that he sees 'very well' 'yonder high hill' to Mr Legality's house. The visible and the immediate become hurdles for the pilgrim who must go through a gate which he is unable to see on the visible level. With the help of Evangelist, Christian sees his error and continues the way 'he must go'.

Seeing on the invisible level keeps Christian through many dangerous experiences resolutely towards his goal. When he asks the men, who 'were almost in the Valley of the Shadow of Death', what they had seen, they reply with astonishment, 'Seen! Why the Valley itself, which is as dark as pitch; we also saw there again Hobgoblins, Satyrs, and Dragons of the Pit...' (p. 62). After listening to the reports of the men, not only of what they had seen but of what they had heard, Christian replies, 'I perceive not yet, by what you have said, but that this is my way to the desired Haven' (p. 62). The men turn away, but Christian goes on from hazard to hazard through the Valley of the Shadow of Death. As he faces 'Snares, Traps, Gins . . . Nets . . . Pits, Pitfalls, deep holes', Christian triumphantly goes through the Valley and clearly shows the focus of his sight when he says, 'His candle shineth on my head, and his light I go through darkness'. The light is the same invisible light of which Evangelist spoke at the beginning of the pilgrimage; and obviously, in the Valley of the Shadow of Death, Christian sees by that light.

Christian fails to see, on occasion, with clarity even after the experiences in the Valley. When he and Hopeful are far along on the journey, they come to the top of a high hill called 'Clear', where they meet shepherds. To see the 'Gates of the Celestial City' can be their joyful experience if they look through the 'Perspective Glass', offered by the shepherds. They look through the glass, but their hands shake as they remember 'the last thing', a byway to Hell, that the shepherds showed them. For fear they will lose sight of the invisible and gain sight of the visible, the pilgrims can only say, as they look through the Perspective Glass, 'they thought they saw something like the Gate and also some of the Glory of the place' (pp. 122–3).

Seeing on an invisible level is a price too costly for many false pilgrims. Atheist, for example, sees no more of the City to which Christian refers than he did the first day he 'set out', and that was 'twenty years before'. In his judgement, his only alternative is to return to his own country, for he says, 'I am going back again, and will seek to refresh my self with the things that I then cast away, for hope of that, which I now see, is not' (p. 135). For Atheist, there is no such place as that toward which Christian and Hopeful travel if it cannot be seen on the visible level.

To summarise, Bunyan relies heavily on the metaphor of sight to separate what can readily be seen from what can be seen through the light of faith. It is the willingness to see by the latter that separates Bunyan's true pilgrim from those who would make the journey only if they can see or perceive each stage.

If there is no problem in seeing the way in which sight metaphor unites the various stages of the dream, there is the possibility that a reader may charge that the dream vision lacks a sequence of causally related events. Freud, for example, questions how logical relations can be exhibited in dreams. He wonders what representation words like 'if ' and 'because' and 'although', and all other conjunctions which we find necessary in constructing sentences, have in dreams. From Freud's point of view, the dream has no way of representing these. We would have to admit that there is a suspension of certain *ordinary* logic as far as the sequence of images is concerned, and that there is little rational causality in *The Pilgrim's Progress* without recourse to allegory. But when we perceive the latent content on dream-thoughts of Bunyan's vision and understand that *The Pilgrim's Progress* exhibits dream-content beyond the framework itself, we have no question concerning the presence of 'allegorical causality'.[26] Besides, a dream state possesses an innate logic of its own.

One unceasing purpose runs through *The Pilgrim's Progress* from the Wicket Gate to the Delectable Mountains to the margin of the River. The narrow way, the strenuous hill, the valley of peril, the city with its persecutions, the multiform dangers of the road, are all facets of the relentless purpose of a man 'baffled to fight better', but ever fighting and pressing on to a specific goal. When we watch the route Christian takes and why he takes it, we begin to see that words like 'because', and 'although', or any other words used in constructing logical sentences are not foreign to John Bunyan's vision within his allegorical dream framework.

A man is clothed in rags *because* his righteousness is as filthy rags; he cries out, 'What shall I do?' *because* he desperately wants to find release from his burden; he goes to the Interpreter's House *because* he needs instruction in Christian teaching; he stops at the House Beautiful *in order to* receive the necessary armour to withstand his spiritual battles; *although* he is on his way to the Celestial City, he ends up in Doubting Castle, *because* he momentarily thinks he might find an easier route; and he finally arrives at the Celestial City *because* he has the proper certificate for entrance. Bunyan carefully charts each step of the way Christian *must* take, and by recourse to allegory, he invests each 'dream-like' event with an Aeneas-like sense of purpose which is collective and cultural on one level, and individual and solitary on another.

Within the dream narrative Bunyan constructs several levels of allegory. There is, of course, the level of the individual pilgrim, who after becoming aware of his lostness, seeks a solution to his predicament and makes the arduous journey from the City of Destruction to the Celestial City. Not only is there the progress of a single pilgrim. As Bunyan suggests, there is a strongly pronounced Biblical level.

The Biblical level follows the major outlines of the Old and New Testaments. Bunyan early links the authority of the Old Testament story of the safe journey of the Israelites with his selected metaphor of the journey. Christian refers to Old Testament history when he identifies himself as 'of the Race of Japheth whom God will persuade to dwell in the Tents of Shem'. Three Shining Ones underscore Christian's identity as a spiritual descendant when they assure him that he is going 'to Abraham, to Isaac, to Jacob, and to the Prophets'. By invoking the wilderness story of the Israelites, Bunyan has a key to unlock the metaphorical journey from the 'wilderness' of this world to the New Jerusalem.

J. Paul Hunter accurately states that the 'parallel between the plight of modern Puritans and ancient Israelites had been established early in the seventeenth century, and Puritan writers exploited this conviction in formulating their metaphors along the particular outlines of the Old Testament account'.[27] Hunter also shows clear understanding of the way these outlines manifest themselves: 'man typically began life in bondage to his sins (Egypt), was redeemed by grace (release by Pharaoh after the miraculous plagues), changed his life course (Red Sea crossing), underwent trials (dissension, hunger, thirst), alternately experienced punishments and rewards for his conduct (manna, slaying of idolators), and finally achieved his heavenly reward (promised land).[28]

If Bunyan depicts the stages of the release from bondage to regeneration and of the trials of Jerusalem, he turns not only to the Exodus for his Biblical guidelines but also to Psalms, Isaiah, and the Song of Solomon (especially as Christian perceives the glory of Canaan — which he sees as early as his visit to the House Beautiful), to Micah (particularly in his victory over Apollyon, as he discerns the paradox of Scripture: 'Rejoice not against me, O mine Enemy! When I fall, I shall arise'), to Job and Amos (when he overcomes the darkness and terror of the Valley of the Shadow of Death), to Proverbs (when Faithful tells Christian of Wanton's temptations and declares of his tempter, 'her steps take hold of Hell'), and to numerous additional references.

Underpinnings from the New Testament also pervade *The Pilgrim's Progress*, and although Old and New Testament sources intermingle throughout, Bunyan finds Biblical sources for the journey from the 'Red Sea crossing' to the New Jerusalem primarily in the New Testament. In turning to both the Old and New Testaments, his allegory follows the pattern which Isabel MacCaffrey suggests: 'Insofar as they deal with the causes of our happiness and unhappiness, allegorical fictions legitimately include, among their metaphorical patterns, images — sometimes called "mythic" — which are sources, rather than instances, of metaphorical discourse.'[29] From the New Testament, however, Bunyan refers to the Gospel of Mark (when Christian meets the Shining Ones at the Cross), to Ephesians (as Christian puts on a fully equipped armour), to Romans (in the triumph over Apollyon) to James (when Christian instructs Faithful on the nature of Talkative's religion), to Matthew (as Christian understands that Christ too went through Vanity Fair), to Hebrews (when Hopeful and Christian hear of the innumerable company of angels in the Heavenly Jerusalem), to Revelation, and to multiple stories and images from the New Testament.

A theological level also pervades the allegory. Coleridge saw *The Pilgrim's Progress* as 'incomparably the best *Summa theologiae evangelicae* ever produced by a writer not miraculously inspired'.[30] Theological thought is the hinge on which the allegory turns, and Bunyan shows this groundplan for Christian's journey without hampering his imaginative art. What he depicts is essentially what most preachers, like Bunyan, would have learned from their

ministers: man is lost, he needs salvation, he will find salvation at
the Cross through repentance of sin and faith in Christ, he grows
in his spiritual life but faces temptation and frequently stumbles,
and ultimately he arrives at the New Jerusalem. Richard L.
Greaves calls the stages: election, calling, faith, repentance, justification, forgiveness, sanctification, and perseverance.[31]

Early in *The Pilgrim's Progress*, the questing pilgrim, a member of
the elect, is set apart from his neighbours by his resolution to leave
the City of Destruction. To be 'set apart' or 'to be elected' is pre-
dominantly the gracious and sovereign act of an omniscient God.
Even though one is among the elect and election is final and
unchangeable, the 'elected' individual must still go through the
various stages on the way from the City of Destruction to the
Celestial City.

Calling includes a personal realisation of the evil of unbelief
and an awareness of a need of Someone or Something greater than
the individual self. Christian is one of the elect; and since he is
elected by God for salvation, he is called upon to leave his evil
ways, his family, and neighbours, and to seek 'Life, Life, Eternal
Life'. Calling is a matter of grace, and Christian soon discovers
that the Law which offers *a* way by Worldly Wiseman is not *the*
way the Grace of God offers. He *must* go by the light of the Word
through the Wicket Gate, the Christ.

After divine grace causes him to heed the calling, another
theological stage surfaces, in that Christian must respond by faith.
Following his informative visit to the Interpreter's House, Christian goes along a wall called Salvation until he comes to the Cross.
At the Cross burdens fall from his shoulders, three shining ones
appear, assure him that his sins are forgiven, give new clothes to
this new man, place a mark on his forehead, and present him a roll
with a seal upon it, which he is to deliver at the gates of the Celestial City. This is a crucial theological stage: a sinner responds in
faith to God's grace and receives the divine reply of forgiveness
and justification. Initiation of grace is the beginning, not the end,
of the pilgrimage, and it is no panacea which guarantees heavenly
bliss for the pilgrim's earthly trek.

The remainder of the journey emphasises the theological level
of sanctification in which Christian perseveres through grace until
the triumphant culmination. Although Christian, and later Faithful and Hopeful, are 'fixed' in salvation, each must persevere unto
death. Christian must endure turmoils of the journey, but

interspersed are varied splendours. Both the struggles and the triumphs are ingredients of the sanctifying process of Christian's arduous journey. What is equally important is that the believer is not without imperfections. Far along the journey and after he has successfully fought numerous battles, Christian meets with clear evidence of little faith and much doubt. Without question, the theological level is yet another possible meaning of the 'literal' text, or more precisely, the literal text embodies the allegorical levels, including the theological, but from the beginning to the end of the journey, the various theological stages are flexible, fading in and out, as they merge to become part of the total pattern of the entire route.

Admittedly, the historical level is less pervasive than the Biblical and theological, but it too is an integral part of the allegory. It has to do not with specific personages by name, as in *The Divine Comedy*, but rather with particular events during the life and era of John Bunyan. It is true, however, that in the references to Old Testament history, Bunyan frequently refers to specific names. When Christian is led into the 'Armoury', for example, he sees Moses' rod, Jael's hammer and nail with which he slew Sisera, Gideon's pitchers, trumpets, and lamps, and David's sling and stone with which he slew Goliath. These Old Testament personages demonstrate in their experiences that the godly pilgrim in any difficult situation can have essential preparation against the enemy. What is of particular solace to the pilgrim is that the history of the Israelites is a prototype of the wilderness journey through which he triumphantly travels to the land of promise. Certainly, the 'Ancient Records' which he saw in House Beautiful would lead Christian to know that many in Biblical history had successfully made the journey.

The historical level again surfaces in the Vanity Fair episode. Bunyan's view of social history, as well as Christian's plight in the contemporary world, emerges in his realistic satire on the ways of the world with its crowded market, particularly in its '*Britain* Row, *French* Row, and *Italian* Row'. As John R. Knott Jr states: 'By reducing secular society to a fair, Bunyan could imply that the collective opinion and power "of all men of the world" are devoted to upholding the economic (and class) system upon which their material well-being is founded.'[32] So uncompromising is Bunyan's view of contemporary society that in the catalogue of merchandise at the fair 'Whores, Bawds, Wives, Husbands, Children, Masters,

Servants' are indiscriminately enumerated among those whose values fail to go beyond the economic or commercial level. When Christian and Faithful refuse to buy anything except truth, they are put in prison and brought before a jury, whose membership includes Mr Blind-Mind, Mr Malice, Mr Love-Lust, and Mr Implacable. In this incident, Bunyan undoubtedly once again turns to contemporary history and recalls the autocratic and arrogant justices, including Sir John Kelynge, Sir Henry Chester, Sir George Blundell, Sir William Beecher, whose taunts he received at his own trial in 1660–1.[33]

Vanity Fair, as a setting for the trial of the two pilgrims and for the martyrdom of Faithful, strongly suggests one of the prominent social places known to Bunyan, the 'Fair Towns' of seventeenth-century England. Even the topography is typical of the mid-seventeenth-century setting of Elstow and Bedford with sloughs, fields, valleys, and meadows.

If the various levels of allegory are figurative interpretations of the literal or metaphorical journey of Christian, so also does 'fictiveness open into vision'[34] at the climax of Part One. The dreamer now sees the pilgrim enter the Celestial City.

> Now just as the Gates were opened to let in the men, I looked in after them; and behold, the City shone like the Sun, the Streets also were paved with Gold, and in them walked many, with Crowns on their heads, Palms in their hands, and Golden Harps to sing praises withall.
>
> There were also of them that had wings, and they answered one another without intermission, saying *Holy*, Holy, Holy, is the Lord. And after that they shut up the Gates; which when I had seen, I wished my self among them. (p. 162)

Isabel MacCaffrey shows keen perception when she states that the images associated with Christian entering the beautiful city exist in a dimension of reality distinct from the earlier images of the Interpreter's House or Doubting Castle; they are not metaphors.[35] What she suggests is that the invented truths of allegory and the achieved truths of vision can inhabit the same story because the author knows the two are complementary. The vision absorbs the figurative into the actuality that stands behind it.[36]

There is also another important facet to this vision that comes at the end of Part I, in that Bunyan now recognises two opposing time factors. The dreamer has followed his pilgrim to the end of his journey and sees him, after manifold struggles, enter the Celestial City. Immediately, the dreamer 'turns his head to look back' and sees Ignorance, who lacks the certificate for entrance, being bound hand and foot and taken away. With an ending characteristic of dream literature, Bunyan simply says, 'So I awoke, and behold it was a dream' (p. 163).

Dream time is over now, and the contemporary is with us. Bedford jail is the reality to which Bunyan awakens. What he does now is to separate the 'dream time' of the allegory from the waking time of the realistic present, both his and ours. Undoubtedly, the emphasis is exactly where Bunyan wants it in order that readers may live in light of the remembered vision. Just as he reminds us in the rhymed preface of the power of allegory to fill the memory, so now Bunyan leaves the burden of proof and of action upon the dream-reader.

That Bunyan is aware of the power of memory is evident in numerous incidents throughout the dream, images by which his readers can recall the essential qualities of the Christian journey. Dante, says Frances Yates, made the entire *Divine Comedy* into a series of mnemonic images inserted into mental places.[37] So also does Bunyan in *The Pilgrim's Progress*. One vivid image is the 'memory room' of the House Beautiful, as the past, present, and future merge. Christian sees 'records of the greatest antiquity' and the 'pedigree of the Lord of the Hill', the Son of 'the Ancient of Days', and the names of hundreds that the Son 'had taken into his service'. He has a view 'of things both ancient, and modern'; he sees among numerous pictures Moses' rod, Jael's hammer and nails, David's sling and stone, but he also beholds the sword which the Lord *will* use to kill 'the man of sin the day that he shall rise up to the prey'. But the picture is incomplete: the man on a journey sees also Immanuel's Land from which he will be able to view the Celestial City. Thus, through memory in his created dream world, Bunyan breaks out of the world of time, and the past and future simultaneously form different parts of the pattern of Christian's tumultuous journey.

One final observation stated in the rhymed preface commands examination: Bunyan's delight in the use of dialogue. That he had thought on the subject is evident: 'I find that man (as high as Trees) will write / Dialogue-wise; yet no Man doth them slight / for writing so' (p. 42).

At times the dialogue is hardly more than stereotyped

conversation; but there are frequent manifestations of a highly dramatic quality. The dialogue between Christian and Mr Worldly-Wiseman has a special excellence. In a few paragraphs, Bunyan reveals the self-satisfaction of Worldly Wiseman, his contempt for Christian's thinking, his bland censure of Evangelist's counsel, and his complacent confidence that Christian's earnestness arises from weakness of the intellect and from following unsound advice. At the same time, Bunyan shows a great deal about Christian: he is not quite prepared for Wiseman's insidious counsel; he is nervous and uncomfortable in the presence of this man of worldly reputation and lacks the discernment to cope with Wiseman's quality of mind.

George Bernard Shaw praises the 'terse manageableness' of the dialogue and the vivid directness in which sentences go straight to the mark.[38] Notice Christian when he leaves the City of Destruction as Obstinate and Pliable try to persuade him to return with them:

Obst. *What are the things you seek*, since you leave all the world to find them?

Chr. I seek an *Inheritance, incorruptible, undefiled, and that fadeth not away*; and it is laid up in Heaven, and fast there, to be bestowed at the time appointed, on them that diligently seek it. Read it so, if you will, in my Book.

Obst. *Tush*, said Obstinate, *away with your Book; will you go back with us, or no?*

Chr. No, not I, said the other; because I have laid my hand to the Plow.

Obst. Come then, Neighbour Pliable, *let us turn again, and go home without him; there is a company of these Craz'd-headed Coxcombs, that when they take a fancy by the end, are wiser in their own eyes than seven men that can render a reason.*

Pli. Then said *Pliable*, Don't revile; if what the good *Christian* says is true, the things he looks after are better than ours; my heart inclines to go with my Neighbour.

Obst. *What! more Fools still? be ruled by me and go back; who knows whither such a brain-sick fellow will lead you. Go back go back, and be wise.* (pp. 11–12)

Not only is the dialogue vividly direct, but it also distinguishes the characters from one another. Obstinate's remarks ring with finality and he *thinks* he needs no help from either people or books; he makes intimidating assertions too about those who do not share his viewpoint. Pliable 'inclines' towards Christian's way, but wavers and turns back when trouble comes. But Christian's terse and direct replies show a resolute person who refuses to turn again to the City of Destruction.

If Bunyan uses dialogue to show the world of action, he just as clearly appropriates it to show states of mind. Christian and Hopeful are miserable pilgrims in Doubting Castle, and their misery comes not exclusively from the brutality of Giant Despair, but from mental torture springing from Christian's thoughtless advice to Hopeful, which leads them to their grim situation. Furthermore, when Giant Despair beats Hopeful and Christian 'without mercy', it is at once evident that Despair's beating is a manifestation of their state of mind, for they have completely forgotten the numerous times mercy has been extended.

Interior dialogues as powerful as the 'To Sell Christ' dialogue of *Grace Abounding* pervade *The Pilgrim's Progress*. One of the most striking is Christian's battle of indecision in the Valley of the Shadow of Death. To be sure, Bunyan does not minimise the horrors of the valley: on the right is a deep ditch; on the left is a dangerous quag; the pathway is narrow, and the darkness prevents his seeing anything except 'the flame and smoke' while the only sounds are 'doleful voices' and 'rushings to and fro'. When Christian comes to a place where he thinks he hears a 'company of fiends' coming to meet him, Bunyan begins at once to show how skilful is his depiction of interior dialogue. He says of Christian:

> . . . he stopt; and began to muse what he had best do. Sometimes he had half a thought to go back. Then again he thought he might be half way through the Valley; he remembered also how he had vanquished many a danger: and that the danger of going back might be much more, than for to go forward; so he resolved to go on. Yet the *Fiends* seemed to come nearer and nearer, but when they were come even almost at him, he cried out with a most vehement voice, *I will walk in the strength of the Lord God*; so they gave back, and came no further. (p. 63)

The 'yet' or 'but' or 'then' might appear on the surface to be stretches of reasoning that suggest a thesis about to reach a conclusion, but closer observation shows that the inner dialogue shifts ground every few seconds, and Christian is waging a battle with indecision. And the indecision continues until he cries out with a 'vehement voice, *I will walk in the strength of the Lord God* '. As stated earlier, the emphasis is exactly where Bunyan wants it: 'upward to the final truth of God, as well as outward to the multiple truths of human life in the middest'.[39]

In the 'Rhymed Preface' and in 'The Conclusion' of Part One of *The Pilgrim's Progress*, John Bunyan justifies his belief in his selected mode; in practice he demonstrates confidence in the truth of metaphysical language and in the transforming power of imaginative art. He knows and he shows that literary art suggests far more than it actually says, and that it shows by indirection, and that metaphor embraces the transcendent and immediate. What he also delineates is the power of imagined language to illuminate with clarity the meaning of reality and thus deepen an awakened understanding of the complexities of facing the significant questions of the tangible, actual world of time and space. The created world of Bunyan's allegory is by design 'out of time', for the 'out of time' and the supernatural are ingredients of a dream-story. Yet the mysterious and infinite work of grace invades the landscape of a pilgrim as he journeys from earth to heaven.

Despite the pundits of literary taste and the diversity of opinion over the literary merits of his work, John Bunyan wrote an allegory that shows literary caution. His utter spontaneity, his fascinating story, his well-balanced structure, his various levels of meaning, his handling of the dream phenomenon, his emphasis on metaphor and memory, his skilful mastery of dialogue, and his shaping each changing stage of a metaphorical journey into a unitary whole, all attest to the strength of Bunyan's literary power. Although his tools are sometimes crude, he writes an allegory that is a continued metaphor, and he writes it in a language notable for its extraordinary felicity.

A few observations should now be made on the Second Part of *The Pilgrim's Progress*, published in 1684 after the publication of *The Life and Death of Mr. Badman* (1680) and *The Holy War* (1682). Part Two is also a journey, covering the same route that Christian travelled. The chief characters are Christian's wife, Christiana, and her children, Mercy, Mr Greatheart, and others who join them. In brief, Part One focuses on the progress of one individual and the route he *must* take; Part Two centres on a group and the route they *do* take as they follow the markers left by Christian.

Part Two lacks the dangers, and perhaps the adventures of Part One. Greatheart protects the travellers and fights the giants for the pilgrims; Mr Skill has immediate medicinal cures for all the diseases that all contract. In fact, places where Christian fought some of his most violent battles become pleasant sojourns for Christiana and her companions. In the Valley of Humiliation, for example, rather than meeting the monstrous Apollyon, the group sees a 'fruitful piece of Ground', a 'fat Ground', a green valley 'beautified with Lillies' (p. 239). Christiana's journey, therefore, has a less interrupted sense of progress even though she follows the same route that Christian travels.

The note of urgency that pervades Part One is also absent. When Christiana, Mercy, and the boys come to the Wicket Gate, the Keeper of the Gate takes Christiana by the hand, leads her through, invites the children in, but Mercy is left without. Mercy fears rejection by the Keeper, but meanwhile on the other side of the Gate, Christiana intercedes for her neighbour and friend. The phrasing of her plea is especially telling:

> *And she said, my Lord, I have a companion of mine that stands yet without, that is come hither upon the same account as myself. One that is much dejected in her mind, for that she comes, as she thinks, without sending for, whereas I was sent, by my Husband's King, to come.* (p. 189)

Obviously there is here no one clothed in rags, with a great burden on his back, breaking out in a lamentable cry, saying, 'What shall I do?' Mercy's reply to the Keeper is equally significant.

When the Keeper opens the gate, discovers her in a swoon, and asks her why she has come, Mercy responds, 'I am come for *that*, unto which I was never invited, as my Friend, *Christiana*, was. *Hers* was from the King and *mine* was from *her*: wherefore I fear I presume.' She further adds: 'And if there is any Grace and Forgiveness of Sins to spare, I beseech that I, thy poor Handmaid, may be partaker thereof.' The Keeper then takes Mercy by the hand, leads her in, and says, 'I pray for all them that believe on me, by what means soever they come unto me' (p. 190). That Bunyan in the Second Part is willing to suggest that the way through the Wicket Gate is now arbitrary, is, of course, contrary to fact; that the tone of the work is more muted and relaxed is equally true. The journey itself is also without haste. Christian stayed three days in House Beautiful; whereas, Christiana and her group stop for a month at the same place and visit for another month with Mr Gaius.

The narrative of the Second Part moves far less rapidly in the first few pages than in Part One. There is a powerful immediacy in the first paragraph of Part One, for in three co-ordinating statements, Bunyan shows the urgency of the action, depicts a synthesis of the various threads of the action, reveals the outline of a man who is the central character in the narrator's dream. Sagacity, on the other hand dominates the beginning of Part Two for about 14 pages, or until the section where the Dreamer thinks he sees 'Christiana and Mercy and the Boys go all of them up to the Gate' (p. 188). What Sagacity does is describe what people in the City of Destruction now think of Christian, what new joys he experiences in the new City, what sorrows Christiana endures because of her insensitivity to her husband, and what decisions she makes for herself and her sons.

Sagacity also reviews the early stages of Christiana's journey, shifts the scene to Mrs Timorous calling in her neighbours for a discussion of the action of 'blind and foolish' Christians; shifts again to Christiana pushing ahead on her journey, with Mercy reluctantly joining her; focuses on conversation of Christiana as she tells of her beginning 'to consider with herself' and then to Mercy as she speaks of things 'within herself'. Bunyan abruptly drops Sagacity with the Dreamer asserting, 'And now Mr. Sagacity left me to Dream out my Dream by myself' (p. 188). For whatever reason Bunyan drops Sagacity from the narrative,[40] there is a new sense of immediacy gained from his absence. It is also true that Bunyan has trouble grasping in the early section of Part Two the potentialities of the dream vision he appropriated so successfully in Part One.

Scenes exhibiting a colloquial style and swift interaction of characters abound in the Second Part. A choice example is a lengthy conversation on fear or 'Mr. Fearing', which occurs among Honest, Greatheart, Christiana, Mercy, Matthew, and James. Furthermore, as suggested, unlike Part One, conversation in Part Two frequently occurs among several participants rather than the usual one-to-one discussions, for example, between Christian and Faithful or Faithful and Talkative or Christian and By-ends.

Utter spontaneity, another characteristic of various characters, is particularly striking when Greatheart and Honest turn the conversation from Mr Fearing to Mr Self-will and his opinions, to opinion in the abstract and back to man and his opinions. Christiana joins in by saying, 'There are strange Opinions in the World. I know one that said 'twas time enough to repent when they came to die' (p. 257).

Another contrasting feature of Part Two is a de-emphasis on doctrinal discussion. Greatheart is the only major character who gives attention to doctrinal implications of acts or deeds, but even Greatheart's discussions with fellow travellers lack the concern over the exposition of Biblical texts and the declaration of Biblical doctrine that the conversation of major characters in Part One manifests. This obvious lack of emphasis on discussions of doctrine leads Charles W. Baird to suggest that even though sentiments and emotions 'externalized through dialogue are concerned with relationship of the human to the divine, they are exclusively so, and that prominence is given to human emotions and sentiments'.[41] That there is solid basis for his judgement may be seen in various stages of the journey, but Christian's human concern over Greatheart's struggle with the Giant is a strong example. After Greatheart slays the Giant, the travellers sit down to rest, to eat and drink, and to celebrate. Discussion follows this order:

As they sat thus and did eat, *Christiana* asked the *Guide, if he had caught no hurt in the battle.* Then said Mr. *Greatheart, No*, save a little on my flesh; yet that also shall be so far from being to my determent, that it is at present a proof of my love to my Master and you, and shall be a means by Grace to increase my reward at last.

But was you not afraid, good Sir, when you see him come with his Club?

It is my duty, said he, to distrust mine own ability, that I may have reliance on him that is stronger than all. *But what did you think when he fetched you down to the ground at the first blow?* Why I thought, quoth he, that so my master himself was served, and yet he it was that conquered at last.

Mat. *When you all have thought what you please, I think God has been wonderful good unto us.* (p. 246)

Characteristically, lengthy expositions are not here; human responses and interactions are in the foreground. This emphasis also seems to support Bunyan's depiction of the place of shared experiences in the Christian journey. Noteworthy also in this thrust is the prominence of music as a means of celebration.

The Keeper of the Gate has a trumpeter 'entertain Christiana with shouting and sound of Trumpet for joy' (p. 189) as she and her company arrive at the Gate. After they come through the Gate and 'walk on in their ways', Christiana begins to sing:

> Bless't the Day that I began
> A Pilgrim for to be;
> And blessed also be that man
> That thereto moved me . . . (p. 193)

After the downfall of Despair, Christiana and Mercy play the viol and the lute, respectively. Even Ready-to-halt leads Much-afraid, 'Dispondencie's Daughter', in a dance. Following Great-heart's discourse on 'Stand-fast', there is a mixture of joy and trembling among the pilgrims, but 'at length they brake out' into song:

> What Danger is the Pilgrim in,
> How many are his Foes . . . (p. 303)

Trumpeters and pipers, with singers and players on stringed instruments welcome the pilgrims as they follow 'one another in at the beautiful Gate of the City'. Musical metaphors, especially the bass and sackbutt, pervade the Second Part. What significance Bunyan attaches to the musical metaphors may be seen from one of Greatheart's speeches:

> . . . Some must *Pipe*, and some must *Weep*: now Mr. *Fearing* was one that play'd upon *this Base*. He and his fellows sound the *Sackbut*, whose Notes are more doleful than the Notes of other Musick are. Tho indeed some way, the Base is the ground of Musick. And for my part, I care not at all for that Profession that begins not in heaviness of Mind. The first string that the Musitian usually touches, *is the Base*, when he intends to put all in tune; God also plays upon this string first, when he sets the Soul in tune for himself. Only here was the imperfection of Mr.

Fearing, he could play upon no other Musick but this, till towards his latter end.

I make bold to talk thus Metaphorically, for the ripening of the Wits of young Readers, and because in the Book of the Revelations, the Saved are compared to a company of Musicians that play upon their *Trumpets* and Harps, and sing their Songs before the Throne. (p. 253)

It is of interest to observe that the base string is an invitation to reconciliation; it gives faith a song of hope. Those who are among 'the Saved' play 'before the throne'; their song belongs to change, transformation and timelessness. One of the most compelling metaphors which surrounds awakening, reconciliation and transformation is music, whether embodied in the dull ballad of Autolycus, the rich songs of Ariel or the songs of the redeemed of John Bunyan. Songs and music comment upon the action at the same time that they are part of it. Music usually heralds a relationship or communication with a supernatural world; frequently, there is an aura of mystery about it, for even the waters in which the travellers bathe suggest sanctification, a cleansing from the soil gathered by travelling.

Closely associated with song is poetry, and Bunyan wrote some of his best in Part Two. It is a harbinger of moments of responsibility, hope, and joy. One of these, the poem of the shepherd boy, is included in the *Oxford Book of English Verse*:

He that is down, needs fear no fall,
He that is low, no Pride:
He that is humble, ever shall
Have God to be his Guide.

I am content with what I have,
Little be it, or much:
And, Lord, Contentment still I crave,
Because thou savest such.

Fulness to such a burden is
That go on Pilgrimage:
Here little, and hereafter Bliss,
Is best from Age to Age. (p. 238)

Equally popular is Valiant-for-truth's 'Who would true valour see', recited just prior to the entrance of the pilgrims into the 'Enchanted Ground'.

The pilgrims of the Second Part also find special delight and entertainment in numerous riddles, a form that Bunyan now uses with considerable adroitness. On occasion he merges the riddle with the emblem as he does in the depiction of the spider in the Interpreter's House, which contains a series of emblematic pictures.

Bunyan saves one of his most artistic sections of Part Two for the last. In prose, or better still poetic prose, Bunyan gives a masterful statement of the glory of belief as the pilgrims cross the river of death. Roger Sharrock calls this passage 'a consciously set piece' and no critic sees more clearly than he what Bunyan does. 'As one by one the pilgrims receive the summons to join their prince across the river', Sharrock says, 'a formalized pattern is repeated with variations: the formula consists of the invitation, an emblematic token of the truth of the message, the bequests of the dying man to his friends, and his last words when crossing the river.'[42] 'The adagio movement' of what goes before throws this 'ordered set piece' into 'bold relief'.[43]

Part Two of *The Pilgrim's Progress*, then, is not without its artistic appeal. Through rapidly moving, progressive scenes, characters vividly reveal themselves as human beings. Emotions, desires, relationships, and joys receive strong emphasis. The metaphorical and allegorical potentialities, however, of familiar images are used less extensively; the inner life is externalised to a great extent through dialogue rather than by allegory. However admirable the may be as narrative, it is not an advancement in Bunyan's allegorical development.

Notes

1. John Stevens, *Medieval Romance* (New York, 1973), p. 240.
2. C.S. Lewis, *Allegory of Love* (New York, 1958), p. 44
3. Richard Blackmur, *The Lion and the Honeycomb* (New York, 1955), p. 131.
4. Isabel MacCaffrey, *Spenser's Allegory* (Princeton, 1976), p. 24.
5. Ibid., n.24.
6. Edwin Honig, *Dark Conceit* (Cambridge, 1960), Chapter III or pp. 57–87 are helpful in showing the shaping of significant allegory.
7. Ibid., pp. 19–50, excellent insights on the nature of symbolic character of allegory.
8. Northrop Frye, *Anatomy of Criticism* (Princeton, 1957), pp. 89–91.
9. 'Letter to Can Grande' *Epistolae* (Oxford, 1966), pp. 199–200. For an excellent,

scholarly explanation of Dante's 'rules' regarding the interpretation of the *Commedia*, see Barbara Reynolds's 'Introduction' in *Paradise, The Divine Comedy* (Baltimore, Penguin Books, 1964), pp. 44–9. Professor Reynolds also clearly shows that allegory, by its very nature, cannot be limited to a twofold interpretation, and she bases her judgement on quotations from the *Convivio, The Epistle to Can Grande,* and *De Monarchia.*

10. In the *Opere Latine Minori,* ed. A.F. Massera (Bari, 1928), p. 216.

11. See rhymed preface to *The Pilgrim's Progress* in *The Pilgrim's Progress,* ed. James Blanton Wharey, revised by Roger Sharrock (Oxford, 1960). All quotations from *The Pilgrim's Progress* are from Wharey's edition.

12. See Michael Murrin, *The Veil of Allegory* (Chicago, 1969), pp. 84–5, for a further discussion of the place of memory in the purpose of allegory.

13. Henry Peacham, *The Garden of Eloquence* (London, 1593), pp 3–4, 13–14.

14. Rhymed preface to *The Pilgrim's Progress,* p. 7.

15. 'Prologue into . . . Leviticus', *Workes* (London, 1573), p. 15.

16. U. Milo Kaufmann, *Traditions in Puritan Meditation* (New Haven, 1966). See especially pp. 3–15.

17. Frye, *Anatomy of Criticism,* p. 90.

18. MacCaffrey, *Spenser's Allegory,* p. 61.

19. Frye, *Anatomy of Criticism,* p. 90.

20. Bunyan's readers would have no trouble linking the Christian pilgrims with the history of the Israelites. This is also another way of putting the authority of the Word behind his central metaphor.

21. Robert Burton, *The Anatomy of Melancholy* (Philadelphia, 1851), p. 103.

22. See Sigmund Freud, *The Interpretation of Dreams* (New York, 1950), pp. 30–43.

23. Erich Fromm, *The Forgotten Language* (New York, 1957), p. 96.

24. Ibid., p. 25.

25. See Harold C. Goddard, 'A Midsummer Night's Dream' in *The Meaning of Shakespeare* (Chicago, 1960), pp. 78–9.

26. Freud, pp. 30–43; and Graham Hough, *A Preface to the Faerie Queene* (New York, 1962), pp. 100–376. *The Pilgrim's Progress* contradicts Hough's statement:

> In much allegory . . . the relation between the two elements (dream conten' dream thought) is quite unlike that found in dreams. In naive allegory, a: in developed religious allegory like *Everyman* or *The Pilgrim's Progress,* the a simple translation of a theme, by a series of one-to-one corresponden element in the theme corresponds to one in the image,

27. J. Paul Hunter, *The Reluctant Pilgrim* (Baltimore, 1966), p. 109.

28. Ibid.

29. MacCaffrey, *Spenser's Allegory,* p. 61.

30. Samuel Taylor Coleridge, *Literary Remains* (London, 1838), III, p.

31. Richard L. Greaves, *John Bunyan,* Courtenay Studies in Reformation (Grand Rapids, 1969), p. 50.

32. John R. Knott Jr., 'Bunyan's Gospel Days: *A Reading of The Pilgrim's Pi* English Literary Renaissance, 3 (1973), p. 451. The entire article is a splendid rea of *The Pilgrim's Progress* with its focus on the metaphor of the 'way'.

33. Roger Sharrock, *John Bunyan* (London, 1954), p. 84.

34. MacCaffrey, *Spenser's Allegory,* p. 65.

35. Ibid.

36. Ibid., pp. 45–8, 59, 66, helpful in understanding more clearly features of 'invented truths' and 'achieved truths'.

37. Frances Yates, 'De umbis idearum' in *The Art of Memory* (Chicago, 1966), pp. 95–6.

38. George Bernard Shaw, *Dramatic Opinions and Essays, The Miscellaneous Writings and Speeches* (London, 1871), p. 359.

39. MacCaffrey, *Spenser's Allegory*, p. 61. See also her footnote on the statement.

40. Henri Talon, *John Bunyan The Man and His Works* (Cambridge, 1951), says that Bunyan 'gets rid of the old man' with 'charming ingenuousness' (p. 155). Sharrock thinks that 'Bunyan's story-teller's instinct prompts him to drop Sagacity with a 'disarming naivete' when he has related Christiana's journey as far as the Wicket-gate' (p. 144). 'Sagacity is abandoned', he says, 'not because Bunyan's intelligence informs him that immediacy is the essence of a dream narration, but because he can now see without him' (p. 142). Charles W. Baird, *John Bunyan. A Study in Narrative Technique* (Port Washington, 1977), thinks that it is possible to see him as evidence of Bunyan's concern for the religious authority of the speaker (p. 38). Baird's views are further stated in footnote 24, pp. 142–3.

41. Baird, *John Bunyan. A Study in Narrative Technique*, p. 92.

42. Roger Sharrock, *John Bunyan*, p. 153.

43. Ibid.

4 THE LIFE AND DEATH OF MR. BADMAN

If *The Pilgrim's Progress* is a narrative of a pilgrim from the City of Destruction to the Celestial City, and if *Grace Abounding* narrates the divine and human significance in the conversion experience of the man, John Bunyan, then *The Life and Death of Mr Badman*, published in 1680, affirms the progressive degradation attendant upon the ungodly man who ignores the conversion experience. *Grace Abounding* and *The Pilgrim's Progress* show man's journey towards God; *Badman* portrays man on a route to damnation. In prophet-like manner Bunyan declares in the preface why he writes the book:

> For that wickedness, like a flood, is like to drown our English world. It begins already to be above the top of the mountains; it has almost swallowed up all; our youth, middle age, old age, and all, are almost carried away of this flood. O debauchery, debauchery, what hast thou done in England! Thou hast corrupted our young men, and hast made our old men beasts; thou hast deflowered our virgins, and hast made matrons bawd. Thou hast made our earth to reel to and fro like a drunkard; it is in danger to be removed like a cottage, yea, it is, because trangression is so heavy upon it, like to fall and rise no more. (p. 6)[1]

With similar urgency, Bunyan passionately maintains that it is the duty of those who can to cry out against this deadly plague of wickedness. Since Bunyan determines to write a work that teaches and since he fills it with copious illustrations of social wrongs that ethical men should avoid, some literary critics hold that the book belongs not to literature but to social history.[2] Admittedly, *Badman* lacks the imagination and the universality of *The Pilgrim's Progress* and certainly has a different thrust from his spiritual autobiography, but it nevertheless shows with a considerable degree of literary merit the life and death of a man who, like Atheist, for instance, of *The Pilgrim's Progress*, refuses to consider the possibility of an existence unbound by the confines of time and space and who ignores the deep implications of man's being created in God's image.

56

That Bunyan's concern has to do primarily not with the literal societal wrongs but with man who should resist the temptations and pressures of the immediate landscape in favour of God who can change both man and society's ills becomes clear in the early part of the work. On the one hand, Bunyan enunciates that 'the ornament and beauty' of the world, 'next to God and his wonders', 'are the men that spangle and shine in godliness'; on the other hand, he shows the life and death of an 'immortal', 'rational', 'sensible being' who considers only that which can be confined within temporal or 'chronos' time. Throughout the entire work, there is an implied contrast between the life man can live and the life God wants him to live, and between a man who recognises the high dignity of being created in God's image and the one who disregards his role 'as the ornament and beauty of this lower world' (p. 7). At the same time, as he unfolds the long list of Badman's wrongs, Bunyan shows that Badman deliberately refuses the option of 'the way he must go' and knowingly chooses the sinful route his life takes. As James Sutherland says, like all Bunyan's writings 'Mr Badman springs from the deepest convictions of the author; he means every word he says . . . He looks on at Mr Badman's spiritual and physical degeneration, missing nothing of what occurs . . . and stating the unwelcome facts with unflinching honesty.'[3]

Bunyan shapes *The Life and Death of Mr. Badman* in the form of dialogue. The dialogue had been used for religious argument in the early history of the church, and Wyclif's appropriation of it in his Latin *Dialogue* and *Trialogus*, of which the first at least was widely read and discussed, had helped to acquaint the reading public with the dialogue as a religious polemic.[4] Furthermore, graphic scenes in Foxe's *History of the Martyrs*, a book which Bunyan knew well, depict dialogues that have all the terseness of reality. The examination of Cranmer, Latimer, and Ridley, the stern questions asked and answered, the denial and contradictions, clearly show a foreshadowing of the doom approaching these men.

Dialogue, then, was not a new form to writers of the seventeenth century, nor was it new to John Bunyan. In early works like *Profitable Meditations*, for example, he appropriates it; and, of course, one of the distinctive literary qualities of *Grace Abounding* and *The Pilgrim's Progress*, as well as other selected works, is strong dialogue. In *Badman* he now chooses dialogue as the literary genre in which to unfold his story, and Bunyan's handling commands examination. He narrates the life and death of his central character, Badman, as two discussants, Wiseman and Attentive, sit under a tree and analyse the notorious Badman. The setting for the dialogue is the same as Arthur Dent's *The Plaine Man's Pathway to Heaven*, which is a colloquy with four participants and which discusses many of the wrongdoings discussed in *Badman*.

To understand, if not fully explain the dialogue, it is essential to think on characteristic qualities of the two conversants. Their names are significant: Wiseman, unlike Wordly Wiseman of *The Pilgrim's Progress*, has knowledge not only of the world but is also a wise believer, schooled in the Puritan ethic and in Biblical theology; Attentive, a neophyte, knows little of the ways of the world and lacks insight into the nature of sin and of human behaviour, and has little understanding of the Bible. What Bunyan suggests through the dialogue between the two participants is that the uninformed, younger Christian, Attentive, must listen and gain knowledge while the older, wiser Christian discusses, teaches, and exhorts. When he permits Attentive to show impatience with Wiseman's lengthy explanations or to show interest in contributing to conversation, Bunyan is able to sharpen the marked difference between the two discussants. During Wiseman's digression, for example, on how those who are bankrupt should deal with their consciences. Attentive finally dares to interrupt, causing the dialogue to proceed in this manner:

> Atten. Well: let us at this time leave this matter and return again to Mr. Badman.
> Wise. With all my heart will I proceed to give you a relation of what is yet behind of his life in order to our discourse of his death.
> Atten. But pray do it with as much brevity as you can. (p. 41)

Not always does Wiseman show understanding toward Attentive's desire for brevity and succinctness, for on another occasion Attentive says, '. . . if you please, let us return again to Mr. Badman himself, if you have more to say of him'. To which Wiseman curtly replies: 'More! We scarce thoroughly begun with anything that we have said' (p. 35). Near the end of the work, Attentive is still impatient but obviously would prefer to avoid Wiseman's rebukes; for when Wiseman interrupts one of his own digressions and suggests that they return to Mr Badman, Attentive in a somewhat obsequious manner remarks 'I think you and I are both of a mind; for just now I was thinking to call you back to him also. And pray now, since it is your own notion to return to him, let us discourse a little more of his quiet and still death.' Wiseman obligingly responds, 'With all my heart' (p. 66). There is also the occasion when Attentive, who is capable of repeating himself, obviously wants the conversation not to be entirely one-sided, makes the dull remark, 'This Badman was a sad wretch', and is cut down by Wiseman's caustic response, 'Thus you have often said before' (p. 45).

The bantering between the two participants underscores the contrast between a well-informed Christian believer and the less-informed but inquiring neophyte, but having conceded this, the dialogue may strike one as unworthy of merit. As Henri Talon states, 'if dialogue is to have didactic value, it should be carried forward briskly and the clash of personalities should cause the sparks to fly to enliven our thoughts'.[5] Admittedly, few sparks fly in the dialogue between the two conversants, but it is only fair to insist that Attentive can quote pertinent biblical references and can show causal relationship among sins, and can do both as readily as Wiseman. In the beginning he dares to disagree with Wiseman. He suggests, for example, that Badman's father should not have given him money to begin his own business, and he argues with Wiseman about the relationship between a father and son. Several hundred words later, Attentive says, 'Well, I yield. But pray let us return again to Mr. Badman' (p. 27). From this point, Attentive seldom openly disagrees, but he shows impatience, asks questions, makes remarks, dull at times, listens fairly closely, and generously acknowledges his debt to Wiseman: 'I also thank you for your freedom of me, in granting of me your reply to all my questions' (p. 69). However monotonous the dialogue may appear, through the explicit and implicit tension between the two speakers, Bunyan is able to sustain the central differences in their personalities as well as in their religious depth. The two never become mere expository instruments. As Charles W. Baird states, 'Wiseman and Attentive generate continued interest and become distinct, lively participants in a drama. They command attention . . . as the dialogue unfolds because of subtle, changing tensions between them.'[6] Bunyan brings this about even though, as Baird also holds, 'their dialogue is undistinguished by individualizing rhythm or "turns" of speech'.[7]

At the centre of the dialogue is, of course, Mr Badman, whom

G.B. Harrison calls a finely drawn character and believes that his portrayal shows what Bunyan could have done had he written Badman's story in pure fiction.[8] Harrison's view is slightly questionable, for most outstanding fictional characters demonstrate strengths and weaknesses; but in *Badman* one turns page after page in quest for some redeeming human grace — a kind act, a thoughtful gesture — anything to disrupt even momentarily the ongoing recital of Badman's wicked deeds. That good and evil 'in the field of this world grow up together almost inseparably' escapes Bunyan's imagination when he draws Badman, but he can clearly show both the magnificence and stupidity of his chief pilgrim in *The Pilgrim's Progress.* In his portrayal of Badman, however, Bunyan reveals not merely an endless catalogue of the central character's sins but rather delineates vivid stages in his degeneration. What might possibly be considered an occasional flash of the wicked man's slight interest in a life different from the one he lives is only barely evident when Badman thinks it might be advantageous to him not to live or to die as an evil man. Never does such fleeting interest eventuate into a deliberate act of the will from which could come a transformed person. He is conceived as Sutherland suggests 'in almost purely animal terms . . . with those added streaks of meanness and grossness and vulgarity to which only humanity can descend'.[9] It is equally true that 'we miss the dignity of spiritual distress which transfigures Bunyan's pilgrims, and makes them walk in garments of shining light even before they reach the Celestial City.'[10] But Bunyan intends that we miss that dignity; his concern is Badman, and through him to show the plain man's pathway to Hell.

From the beginning of his life, Badman possesses an unusual amount of original corruption; as a little child he is notorious for his defiance of his father's instruction, especially in his penchant for lying, stealing, swearing, and cursing. Bunyan shapes the early and later sins into successive steps: a rebellious son, an irresponsible apprentice, an indiscreet tradesman, an unfaithful husband, a fraudulent bankrupt, a clever extortioner, a proud hypocrite and so on through sin after sin until he dies an unrepentant sinner. That he wants a particular order to the stages of Badman's sin and that he bases his selected order on principle is clear from the statement Bunyan gives to Wiseman concerning Badman's pride:

I might at first have begun with Mr. Badman's pride, only I

think it is not the pride in infancy that begins to make a difference betwixt one and another, as did, and do those wherewith I began my relation to his life: therefore I passed it over; but now, since he had no more consideration of himself... but to be proud when come to years, I have taken the occasion, in this place, to make mention of his pride. (p. 49)

Bunyan obviously believes that beginning with concrete sins rather than with the abstract sin of pride will permit him to show more clearly the contrast 'betwixt one another', or between the repentant and the unrepentant sinner — which is a prime reason for writing about Badman in the first place.

Bunyan further emphasises the development of the successive stages in Badman's life by occasionally establishing a causal relationship. In addition to his 'being polluted with original sin', Wiseman speaks of three associates, who would commonly 'egg' him to the ale-house, but yet make him 'Jack-pay-for-all' and who would borrow money from him and never repay it, thus helping to reduce him to poverty. Furthermore, his three acquired 'evil companions', one given to uncleanness, another to drunkenness, and the third to stealing, influence him towards promiscuity. What Bunyan stresses is not that temptations reduce Badman to a pawn in the tempter's hands, but rather that he is unlikely to hear and to know of the meaning of godly living if he spends all of his time with sinful companions. In Bunyan's thinking, to understand the 'ornament and beauty of this lower world . . .' entails associates unlike Badman's friends. If Bunyan shows successive stages in Badman's sins and if he demonstrates causal relationships among the stages, so similarly he does effectively combine various aspects of Badman's nature into a composite picture, reminiscent of seventeenth-century character sketch, a genre developed particularly by Overbury, Earle, and Fuller. Near the close of the work, for example, Wiseman says, 'But what need I thus to talk of the particular actions, or rather the prodigious sins of Mr. Badman, when his whole life, and all his actions, went, as it were to the making up one massy body of sin?' (p. 52). Summary statements of Badman's actions also show facets of his character: when God manifests mercy, Badman ascribes the source of his own wit, or care; when crosses come, he attributes them to chance, 'ill management of matters', or to his wife's religion, and instead of reverencing scripture, he objects to its 'authority, harmony, and wisdom', or instead of loving and honouring Christians, he makes them objects of slander. In a cogent character sketch, Wiseman concludes:

> He was an angry, wrathful, envious man, a man that knew not what meekness or gentleness meant, nor did he desire to learn. His natural temper was to be surly, huffy, and rugged, and worse; and he so gave way to his temper, as to this, that it brought him to be furious and outrageous in all things, especially against goodness itself, and against other things too, when he was displeased . . . then was Mr. Badman, notwithstanding the conceit that he had of his own abilities, a fool of no small size . . . Mr. Badman was a malicious and as envious a man as you commonly hear of. (p. 53)

These terse, pithy statements show with clarity the sketch of a man without intellectual, moral, and religious inclinations.

Not only does the dialogue show the character of Badman but also depicts an important female character, the first Mrs Badman. Initially Wiseman and Attentive seem to discuss her merely as an illustrative example of troubles awaiting the believer who marries an unbeliever, but her statements and interior monologues, along with the numerous manifestations of her stress and pain, ultimately suggest a rather complex character. Charles W. Baird states that she speaks for herself often enough to become the first complex character in Bunyan's narrative.[11] What emerges early in the dialogue regarding Mrs Badman is her deep hurt over the existing conflict between her love for her husband and her concern for her own soul's salvation. In a reversed pattern of Shakespeare's Hermia but just as straightforwardly, she says, 'You are commanded to love me, as you love your own body, and so do I love you; but I tell you true, I prefer my soul before all the world, and its Salvation will I seek' (p. 33). Through all her trials with her unbelieving husband, she uncompromisingly and consistently retains her position: she loves him, she loves their children, and wants the children to respect their father, but the salvation of an individual's soul is of prime significance.

When she knows that her death is near she reminds Badman of her fidelity, of his abuses of her, and of his need to forsake his wrongdoing. In rather lively, brisk words for a dying person, she says to her husband:

God knows, and thou shalt know, that I have been a loving, faithful wife unto thee; my prayers have been many for thee; and as for all thy abuses that I have received at thy hand, those I freely and heartily forgive, and still shall pray for this conversion, even as long as I breathe in this world. But husband, I am going thither, where no bad man shall come, and if thou doest not convert, thou wilt never see me more with comfort; let not my plain words offend thee: I am thy dying wife, and of my faithfulness to thee, would leave this Exhortation with thee: Break off thy sins, fly to God for mercy while mercies gate stands open . . . (p. 58)

These final expressions of concern and exhortation clearly unfold not only Bunyan's imaginative comprehension of Mrs Badman's marital predicament, but also show that such a state fails to lessen her sensitivity to Badman's supreme need. Further, her exemplary Christian life, her concern for her family, her disavowal of earthly values, and her preparation for death slacken Bunyan's emphasis on her pain and, at the same time, sharpens the contrast he frequently implies between the repentant and the unrepentant sinner. Baird states:

Her death is presented as exemplary in that she exhibits joyful anticipation of her future home ... and even a certain eagerness to use the emotional maturity her situation gives her to encourage her family's reformation . . . and the elaborate, almost ritualistic, preparation for death establishes a norm in light of which Mr. Badman's ignoble end is to be seen.[12]

If the dialogue between Wiseman and Attentive depicts the various facets of individuals, so also does it show the characteristics of the age in which a character like Badman lives. Almost everything connected with humanity acquires a stench, and especially vicious to Bunyan are those practices which are convenient instruments for the exploitation of the poor. 'Extortion,' says Bunyan, 'is screwing from men more than by the law of God or men is right' (p. 45); it is an evil committed by men in office in regard to fees, rewards, and the like, but Bunyan contends that it is most prevalent among tradesmen. And in a telling indictment, he vividly demonstrates the manner in which extortion pervades the world of Badman:

We have a great many people in the country too that live all
their days in the practice, and so under the guilt of extortion;
people, alas! that think scorn to be so accounted. As for example:
there is a poor body that dwells, we will suppose, so many miles
from the market; and this man wants a bushel of grist, a pound
of butter, or a cheese for himself, his wife, and poor children;
but dwelling so far from market, if he goes thither, he shall lose
his day's work, and will be eightpence or tenpence damage to
him, and that is something to a poor man. So he goeth to one of
his masters or dames for what he wanteth, and asks them to
help him with such a thing. Yes, say they, you may have it; but
withal they will give him a gripe, perhaps make him pay as
much, or more, for it at home, as they can get when they have
carried it five miles to a market, yea, and that too for the refuse
of their commodity . . . Now this is a kind of extortion, it is a
making a prey of the necessity of the poor, it is a grinding of
their faces, a buying and selling of them. But above all, your
hucksters, that buy up the poor man's victuals by wholesale,
and sell it to him again for reasonable gains, by retail. (p. 45)

For hucksters and all other middlemen Bunyan has a thorough
distrust, and his business ethic always favours the needs of the
consumer before the desires or ambitions of the producer. Bunyan
apparently believes the establishing of prices to be a controversial
subject, for Attentive, thoroughly perplexed over the subject of
buying and selling, reminds Wiseman that 'there is no settled price
set by God upon any commodity that is bought or sold', but the
core of Wiseman's response suggests three principles for both the
one who buys and the one who sells: conscience to God, charity to
neighbour, and much moderation in dealing. Central to Bunyan's
position is his belief that making money without working for it
militates against the building of a strong Christian character. But
it is the plight of the poor which tears at Bunyan; it is they who are
'ground down', 'bought and sold', through the ruthless practices of
the extortioners.

Usury[13] is also denounced; again, it is the poor who suffer and
Wiseman says:

What would you say if I should anatomize some of those vile
wretches called pawnbrokers, that lend money and goods to poor
people, who are by necessity forced to such an inconvenience;

and will make by one trick or other the interests of what they so lend amount to thirty, forty, yea, sometimes fifty pounds by the year; notwithstanding the principal is secured by a sufficient pawn. (p. 46)

Combined with the grinding down of the poor are other evils that become objects of Bunyan's attack: immorality, marriages of believer with unbeliever (particularly seen in Mrs Badman's story), sabbath breaking, hypocrisy, carnality, whoring, the non-existence of ethical standards, and a whole host of other imprudent and evil practices, all becoming the butt of his invective. Juxtaposed with the diatribes is an acute awareness of man as victim — particularly, of course, the poor man, who is whipped about to support the shibboleths of property, authority, and power. But, a wicked man like Badman is agent far more than victim of the evils that crush and divide, and Bunyan refuses to relieve his 'anti-hero' of responsibility for his wrongdoings.

In order, however, to underscore the relation between 'bad men' and a 'bad world', Bunyan frequently has Wiseman and Attentive tell anecdotes. There are some 20 of these interspersed throughout the dialogue, some told with extraordinary conciseness. Wiseman and Attentive add an authenticity to the anecdotes by beginning them with 'I saw' or 'I read', thus giving the effect that the events are not merely illustrations but rather are in the forefront of the narrative. It is not unusual for the anecdotes to contain satirical barbs, such as the one on fornication, which is also excellent for the way in which it shows the fierce pace of sin in courtly society:

Now there was made in the room hard by a very great fire; so the gentleman took up the babe, went and drew the coals from the stock, cast the child in and covered it up and there was an end of that. (p. 23)

More elaborately presented than this is the story of Dorothy Mately, a perjurer and an inhabitant of Ashover in the country of Derby, who stole money from a fellow worker in a sand-pit, and on denying the charge was sucked into the ground and suffocated. The lad from whom Dorothy Mately stole the money had 'laid his breeches by and was at work in his drawers'. From this pseudo-comic note, Bunyan begins to pile up circumstantial evidence, states exact sum, precise length of time, until he shows the definite judgement on Dorothy Mately for her perjury: 'A great stone fell upon her head, and broke her skull, and then the earth fell in upon her and covered her' (p. 16). The account of Dorothy Mately, expanded from a rather meagre version in Samuel Clark's *A Mirrour and Looking-glass for both Saints and Sinners*, not only gives authority to Bunyan's story but discloses his compelling belief that evil brings death and judgement.

If Bunyan uses specific data and locates his anecdotes in time and place, so similarly does he construct series of intensely realistic descriptions, sometimes with equally intense crudity. The story of John Cox, a man who lives in Brafield and murders himself after a long illness, shows the coarse vitality of some of the dialogue. Posing as a weary man who needs rest, John Cox requests his wife to leave his sick room, but instead of sleeping, he reaches for his razor and cuts a big hole in his side:

> out of which he pulled and cut off some of his guts, and threw them with the blood, up and down the chamber . . . When he had turned him of his back to the wall, the blood ran out of his belly as out of a bowl, and soaked quite through the bed to the boards, and through the chinks of the boards it ran pouring down to the ground'. (p. 65)

After adding crude details of physical dissolution, Bunyan insists on the credibility of his anecdote by stating that the story came from an eyewitness and by declaring that he has available many additional pertinent details which he withholds. Undoubtedly few regret his restraint, but it is still true of literature that life and experience in all its problematic, muddy, and human reality can be the focus of realism as well as of seriousness and sublimity.

The anecdote which is most attractive is the tale of Old Tod, the thief who repented and gave himself up to the court. Without accumulation of circumstantial details and without the ugliness of dreadful physical disintegration, Bunyan permits the anecdote to tell its own story:

> . . .while the judge was sitting upon the bench, comes this Old Tod into the court, clothed in a green suit, with his leathern girdle in his hand, his bosom open, and all on a dung sweat, as if he had run for his life; and being come in, he spoke aloud as

follows: 'My Lord,' said he, 'here is the veriest rogue that breathes upon the face of the earth. (p. 11)

The sudden entrance, the physical detail, the dramatic remorse, the urgent confession, all artistically related, clearly enunciate the author's conviction that confession of sin is essential if man is to evade the life and death of Badman, even though Badman dies 'like a chrisom-child'. What is especially important is that Bunyan moulds his numerous anecdotes into effective stories, tells some of them with a commendable degree of imagination, and weaves each of them into the forefront of the narrative in order to show the horrors of living without the transformation of divine grace in a human life.

Embedded within the dialogue is the idiomatic expression, which is characteristic of all of Bunyan's writings. Other seventeenth-century writers, whose high style Bunyan is unable to reach write expressions with a colloquial and homely grace. John Donne, for example, chooses, on one occasion, a commercial image to clarify the sinful nature of man in his tendency to sell himself to Satan in his day-to-day sins. With considerable wit, he says, 'In Adam we were sold in grosse; in our selves we are sold by retail.'[14]

The Life and Death of Mr Badman shows little of the style reached by the educated mind of the Dean of St Paul's, but Bunyan still skilfully uses the idiomatic expression to underscore the condition of sinful man in a sinful world and at times to show the relationship of the world here to the heavenly world. He finds rich quarry in various sources: the bird in the air knows not the bird in the snare; better never profess, than to make profession a stalking-horse to sin; there is a snake in the grass, a worm in the gourd; the Lord's Day is a kind of Emblem of the heavenly Sabbath above; Jades there be of all colours; if this be bad in the whole, it is also bad in the parts.

In addition to the colloquial idioms and proverbial expressions of the dialogue, Bunyan frequently appropriates with strong effect the figure, anaphora — the device of repeating a word or phrase at the beginning of successive clauses or sentences: 'If they railed on good men, so could he; if they railed on religion, so could he; if they talked beastly, vainly, idly, so would he; if they were for drinking, swearing, whoring or any of the like Villanies, so was he' (p. 35). In referring to lax principles attending marriage between believers and unbelievers Bunyan shows another excellent use of anaphora, he says, 'Soon after such marriages, conviction, the first step toward heaven, hath ceased; prayer, the next step toward heaven hath ceased; hungerings and thirstings after salvation, another step towards the kingdom of heaven, hath ceased' (p. 32).

For all the uniqueness and colour the various idiomatic expressions and literary figures lend to the medium, Bunyan, like other seventeenth-century writers, is noted for his prolixity. To find alternative ways of examining a word and to wring every possible meaning from it is characteristic of *Badman*:

> Now thus to break is to defraud, that is, deceive and beguile; which is as you see forbidden by the God of Heaven . . . It is a kind of theft and robbery, thus to defraud and beguile. It is . . . a thing odious to reason and conscience . . . It is a designed piece of wickedness. (p. 38)

Although most writers of the seventeenth century buttress their views with copious quotations from the Bible, the Classics, the medieval books and selected works of their contemporaries, the unlearned but not illiterate tinker, primarily supports his persuasions with abundant quotations from the Old and New Testaments and from his personal observations. With each writer this prolixity is in part his attitude towards the immanent and the transcendent; it is an outward manifestation of the inward fervency of his beliefs.

Whereas metaphors, similes, analogies, and paradoxes are literary devices characteristic of most seventeenth-century writings, it is the simile, or comparison, that most frequently offers Bunyan a means of achieving concreteness and immediacy. The simile assists, for example, in giving Bunyan a way of seeing relationships in Badman's wickedness: 'I do think it was delightful to Mr Badman to hear, raise, and tell lies and lying stories of them that fear the Lord, as it was for him to go to bed when a weary' (p. 53). Mr Badman 'was so envious an one . . . that he would swell with it as a toad . . . swells with poison' (p. 54).

But with all the contrasts, anecdotes, idiomatic expressions, and similes, Bunyan's narrative of Badman contains sections of dialectical precision, and nowhere is the tool more evident than when Wiseman argues from the major premiss that good 'conscience, reason and nature' must be the basis for both buying and selling. After winding through his somewhat intricate arguments it is obvious that the three key words of this premise sum up Bunyan's demand of mankind whether it is in the isolation of man's heart or in the traffic of the marketplace.

To clarify what Bunyan does as imaginative writer in the Dialogue does not exclude a recognition of some of its weaknesses. Admittedly, Wiseman and Attentive too frequently converse from the same point of view, with Wiseman doing most of the talking and with Attentive asking the 'right' questions at the right time and agreeing with Wiseman's explanations or adding an unnecessary remark. During the account of Badman's breaking his leg, for example, Wiseman informs Attentive that Badman broke his leg when he came home drunk from the ale-house. Attentive simply responds, 'Did he break his leg then?' and follows with 'Pray how did he break it?' When Wiseman explains Badman's drunken bout at the ale-house, his ride towards home, his horse throwing him, his breaking his leg, his swearing and subsequent praying, Attentive merely extends Wiseman's discourse with the expected statement, 'And then you say he called upon God.' After Wiseman's speculation on whether the central character called on God because he wanted to get rid of the pain in his leg or to get cleansing for the sins of his soul, Attentive merely mutters out into the air like a pseudo-Chekhovian character, 'It was a wonder he did not break his neck' (pp. 54-5). Although this section of *Badman* commands little praise, the speakers do not disintegrate into mere rhetorical or expository instruments. On the contrary, Wiseman and Attentive generate continued interest and become distinct, lively participants in a drama.[15]

Furthermore, the book in its entirety is by no means deprecated by the critics. Jack Lindsay, for example, calls it the first realistic novel[16] and Maurice Hussey finds it of interest that Arthur Dent should exert such strong influence on this 'modern novel.'[17] Bonamy Dobrée understands both the strengths and weaknesses of Bunyan's prose in *Badman*, and in one succinct statement he crystallises an accurate view: 'It is well shaped and muscular; it can do with precision what it sets out to do. It disdains nothing and is afraid of nothing. It speaks with the directness and candour of the cottage fireside.'[18] Bunyan clearly shows in *Badman* what evil does in man and in the world and he does it in a style distinctly his own: 'The voice with the Biblical intonation . . . lover of the plain phrase.'[19]

Notes

1. All quotations from *The Life and Death of Mr. Badman* are from *The Entire Works of John Bunyan*, ed. Henry Stebbing (London: James S. Virtue, 1861), IV.

2. Talon contends in *John Bunyan The Man and His Works* (Cambridge, 1951) that the book is inseparable from the period in which it was written and that it throws light on the history of the Puritan seventeenth century. Hence its value is primarily historical (p. 239).

3. James Sutherland, *English Literature of the Late Seventeenth Century* (Oxford, 1969), p. 334.

4. Elizabeth Merrill, *The Dialogue in English Literature* (New York, 1911), p. 44.

5. Talon, *John Bunyan The Man and His Works*, p. 237.

6. Charles Baird, *John Bunyan, A Study in Narrative Technique*, p. 77.

7. Ibid., p. 76.

8. G.B. Harrison, *John Bunyan, A Study in Personality* (London, 1928), p. 154.

9. James Sutherland, *English Literature of the Late Seventeenth Century*, p. 334.

10. Ibid.

11. Baird, *John Bunyan, A Study in Narrative Technique*, p. 80.

12. Ibid., p. 81.

13. Sharrock and others suggest that Bunyan's business ethic retains many medieval features; and though this may be true, C. S. Lewis has a most provocative thought on usury. See *Mere Christianity* (London, 1952):

> There is one bit of advice given to us by the ancient heathen Greeks, and by the Jews in the Old Testament, and by the great Christian teachers of the Middle Ages, which the modern economic system has completely disobeyed. All these people told us not to lend out money at interest; and lending money at interest — what we call investment — is the basis of our whole system. Now it may not absolutely follow that we are wrong. Some people say that Moses and Aristotle and the Christians agreed in forbidding interest (or 'usury' as they called it), for they could not foresee the joint stock company, and were only thinking of private moneylenders, and that, therefore, we need not bother about what they said . . . But I should not have been honest if I had not told you that those great civilizations had agreed (or so it seems at first sight) in condemning the very thing on which we have based our whole life. (p. 67)

14. *The Sermons of John Donne*, 10 vols., eds. George R. Potter and Evelyn Simpson (Berkeley, 1953-62), II, p. 115.

15. Baird, *John Bunyan. A Study in Narrative Technique*, p. 77

16. J. Lindsay, *John Bunyan, Maker of Myths* (Port Washington, NY, 1937, reprinted 1969), p. 209.

17. M. Hussey, *Variety of Ways* (Oxford, 1932), p. 44.

18. Bonamy Dobrée, p. 42.

19. 'Arthur Dent's Plain Mans Path-way to Heaven', *Modern Language Review*, 44 (1949), 33. (The anticipation of eighteenth-century writers, and of Defoe in particular, has been exaggerated by writers like Edmund Gosse, *A History of Eighteenth Century Literature* (London, 1889), p. 85. Sharrock, pp. 116-19 and Talon, pp. 234-5 give a more balanced view.)

5 *THE HOLY WAR*

Critics castigate *The Holy War* for being a 'magnificent failure'[1] and praise it for being so excellent that 'if *The Pilgrim's Progress* did not exist, *The Holy War* would be the best allegory ever written'.[2] Varieties of attitude prevail between these polarities.

John Tullock says: 'It neither seizes upon the imagination nor touches the heart as the story of Christian does. Singularly ingenious, elaborate, and coherent in its illustrations and characters, it is almost as great a marvel, but is not nearly so felicitous nor exquisite a product of genius.'[3] G.B. Harrison thinks of *The Holy War* as 'a most elaborate and ingenious allegory' and further states that it is 'for that very reason less successful as an appeal to conscience than *The Pilgrim's Progress*, because the reader is compelled all the time to admire the astonishing ingenuity of the author'. In Harrison's view, however, 'as a work of art,' *The Holy War* is 'the greatest English allegory'.[4] C.S. Lewis contends that while it is true that the *bellum intestinum* is the root of all allegory, it is no less true that only the crudest allegory will represent it by a pitched battle'.[5] He further holds that *The Pilgrim's Progress*, built on the outlines of a journey, is a better book than *The Holy War* with warfare or combat as the informing metaphor. 'The journey has its ups and downs, its pleasant resting-places enjoyed for a night and then abandoned, its unexpected meetings, its rumours of danger ahead, and, above all, the sense of its goal . . .' says Lewis, and that 'represents far more truly than any combat in a *Champ Clos* the perennial strangeness . . . and the sinuous forward movement of the inner life'.[6] James F. Forrest, editor of a splendid edition of *The Holy War*, refuses to accept the restrictive nature of the military metaphor. He holds that in the

> fortunes of war, sudden alarums and excursions may often give place to quiet diplomacy, lengthy negotiations, truces, uneasy peaces between hostilities — to periods, in short, when tension is markedly relaxed, and when the allegorist, if he so chooses, can conveniently deal with the underside of the moral life, triumph, as well as defeat, hope and joy, as well as despair and anguish.'[7]

Forrest further believes that, among other reasons, *The Holy War* is 'to be appreciated for its mythic power', and that it is 'to be treasured as a fine work of art'.[8]

The critical spectrum suggests that *The Holy War* exhibits a full and perhaps overly elaborate exploitation of the allegorical method that Bunyan previously used. To get at the nature of the allegory through a critical examination of the work is a greater concern of mine than to enter into evaluative criticism. That Bunyan, however, uses one of the oldest and most popular figures of the Christian tradition as his defining metaphor is evident from a cursory glance at works based on warfare metaphors.

The warfare metaphor appears at least as early as the fifth-century *Psychomachia* of Prudentius. Around AD 1200, it appears in the handbook, *Ancrene Riwlg*, in Lydgate's Assembly of Gods (*c.* 1440), and in his translation of the fourteenth-century poem, Guillaume de Deguilleville's *Le Pelerinage de l'Âme. The Castell of Perseverance* (*c.* 1425), and later, Spenser's depiction of the siege of the House of Alma include warfare as controlling metaphor.

In the seventeenth century, John Downame in *The Christian Warfare* (1612), William Gouge in *The Whole Armour of God* (1616) and Richard Bernard in *The Isle of Man* (1627) are among the numerous writers who appropriate the warfare metaphor. The Bible, the book which Bunyan knew best, shows numerous references to spiritual battles in which the believer is engaged, including the struggle within ('the flesh against the Spirit and the Spirit against the flesh' Gal. 5:17), and the forces without ('principalities and powers', Rom. 8:38). Not only does Bunyan write, then, in a reputable and familiar tradition, but also in a mode, as he argued earlier, which has behind it the authority and example of the Scriptures.

In this allegory, however, Bunyan indicates no compulsion to convince his readers that he is writing in a legitimate medium; rather, he seems more concerned, as indicated in 'An Advertisement to the Reader' (p. 286), that readers have no doubt concerning his being the author of *The Holy War*. There is, nevertheless, no indication that Bunyan departs in any way from his early convictions that the primary attribute of allegory is to entice the reader to further imaginative and thoughtful exploration, to rectify the mind, to produce pleasure, to make the will submit and to train the mind.

The central metaphor of *The Holy War* defines the nature of man's soul in terms of two antagonistic powers, and all the unfolding action of the allegory asserts the significance and centrality of the struggle between them. The focus, however, is a town in which struggles embrace battles which touch the individual soul, the loss of Paradise, Old and New Testament events and personages, seventeenth-century England, and the future of man. Bunyan uses the central metaphor and subordinate literary devices to tell his story of *The Holy War.*

Absent from *The Holy War* is the dream phenomenon with the Dream-Narrator. As Roger Sharrock states, after 'the first paragraph, the "I saw", "I behold" of the visionary, so constant in the early allegory, are absent',[9] but the observer-auditor narrator does not as he seems to suggest, disappear after the first paragraph. He frequently, but quietly, asserts his presence by such statements as 'I dare say, Diabolus, their king, had in these days his rest much broken' (p. 61); or 'In these days, as I was informed, new thoughts, and thoughts that began to run counter one to another, began to possess the minds of men of the town of Mansoul' (p. 61); or 'Well, I told you before how the prisoners were entertained by the noble Prince Emmanuel, and how they behaved themselves before him ...' (p. 122); or, 'And I made great observation of it, that so long as all things went in Mansoul as this sweet-natured gentleman Captain Credence would, the town was in most happy condition' (p. 170); or 'Now, if you have not forgot, you may yet remember that I told you before, that after Emmanuel had taken Mansoul there remained ... many of the old Diabolonians' (p. 183).

Through his numerous statements in the first person, this narrator, who moves through time and space, gives an immediacy and a unity to the epic-like structure of the allegory as it shifts from earth to heaven to hell, to battlefields, and into the inner thoughts of individuals. What the narrator emphasises becomes a guideline, or a rule, by which the allegory is to be understood. Charles W. Baird believes that the narrator suggests 'an interpretation most directly through concise summaries that end separate phases of the action', but Baird also believes that this narrator is 'less inimical to an illusion' because his 'most direct textual interpretation suggestions point inward to the text itself rather than outward to external actualities'.[10] What Bunyan primarily does through the narrator is to show one of his designed rules for comprehending his work, a practice not limited to Bunyan or to allegorists. As Isabel McCaffrey accurately states, 'Every successful literary work teaches us the rules by which it is to be understood. The allegorist does this in a particularly self-conscious way ... '[11] While she does insist that allegory is an analytic mode, she does not mean, as she later suggests, that the allegorist, who designedly indicates the relationship of his images to precepts and examples, inhibits 'the richness of interpretive potentiality'.[12]

From the narrator's directions and from the unfolding of every stage of the action, it is evident that the allegory moves on several levels at once, though not equally present at all times. The most pervading level is that of the town of Mansoul as the individual man, elected by God for salvation, wars within his soul to follow Christ's (Emmanuel's) command or to heed the claims of the devil (Diabolus). To begin his allegory, Bunyan shifts back in time to the story of the fallen angels, a warfare led by Diabolus, a once 'great and mighty prince'. This mighty Tempter wants the soul and heart of man even though Shaddai (God) created man in his creaturely, God-like glory only for Himself. Diabolus invades man's soul, blinds his understanding, and conquers his will. Emmanuel attacks the town of Mansoul and pleads for the sinful individual, elected for Salvation, to resist Diabolus. What Bunyan begins to do on this level of his allegory is to show not only how deeply God yearns for man to trust Him but also to depict how serious is the warfare for man's soul.

After Emmanuel's first attack on the town, sinning man, through faith, recognises the nature of his sin, repents in sorrow, and seeks forgiveness. In the pardon of Mansoul by Emmanuel, sinful man receives mercy and justification. In the cleansing of Mansoul and the trial of the Diabolonians, Bunyan shows the need for closer union with Emmanuel. Not only is there the cleansing of Mansoul, but also the people of Mansoul seek to imitate Emmanuel's walk, to feast on food 'that came from his Father's court', (p. 131) and to hear expositions of 'curious riddles of secrets' (p. 132).

The warfare is not over, however, for Mansoul succumbs to the 'venom in the flattering words' of Mr Carnal Security, who succeeds in dulling Mansoul's love for Emmanuel. Suffering ensues as the Diabolonians and the Army of Doubters battle with Emmanuel for the soul of man. Although pardon comes again, the individuals of Mansoul have discovered the constancy of warfare for the persevering believer, elected for salvation.

The various events fall into a general pattern of the seven stages of the Puritan conversion experience, which, as stated in the previous chapter, Greaves calls: election, calling, faith, repentance, justification, forgiveness, sanctification, and perseverance.[13] It is obvious, therefore, that the personal or individual level meshes with a theological level throughout the allegory.

Like contrapuntal technique in music, other levels of allegory often emerge for a while, submerge and then regain prominence, but as the action unfolds, each will fuse at some point with the primary level, with all levels finally telling one story. To sort out these various levels presents difficulties for a critic, for if we follow this route, as James F. Forrest recognises, we are 'compelled to articulate a complex imaginative experience that is readily inexpressible in terms other than the artist's own. Paradoxically, the more the critic succeeds in laying bare the particular layers, the more he fails to give an accurate account of the allegory in general.'[14] Without isolating possible levels or pushing any to the extreme, it is wise to observe the prominence of other emphases.

Early in the preface or 'Note to the Reader', Bunyan directs the reader to the Biblical level and states that no one doubts the troubles of Mansoul 'that are acquainted with those histories/That Mansoul and her wars anatomize' (p. 2). His marginal note reads 'The Scriptures.' In the beginning of the allegory proper, Bunyan tells his story of the Genesis account of Satan (Diabolus) who tempts Adam (Mansoul) to fall and to disobey God (Shaddai).

The Biblical allegory also emerges with the attack of the four captains of Shaddai: Boanerges, Conviction, Judgement, and Execution. Each of these captains is, of course, caught up in the design of the story, but they seem, as Daniel Lamont suggests, to point to the 'Law as an antecedent to the Gospel'.[15] Certainly, they are unable to save Mansoul, which is in harmony with Biblical references that the Law fails in itself to bring salvation. With the entrance of Emmanuel and his victory, there is yet another biblical level. When he brings in the Lord High Secretary or the holy Spirit to reside within man, Bunyan focuses on the biblical story. The warfare with Carnal Security surely suggests the Pauline teaching of the struggle within man between the flesh and the spirit.

Warfare on the historical level *may* be present, but distortions of this level easily occur, especially if one insists on chronological accuracy. William York Tindall, for example, thinks of Diabolus' first reign in Mansoul as an allegory for the rule of Charles I, only to admit that the features are similar to those of Charles II.[16] If

Tindall is searching for parallels, he should have followed his hunch. It seems unlikely that Bunyan could have restrained his criticism of Charles II. Perhaps Bunyan includes on the historical level some of his own experiences, especially the allegorising of his experiences before the English courts in the ludicrous trial scene.

On a political level, there is some allegorical support for the rule of the fifth Monarchists. As tenuous as the evidence is, Tindall could have a point in suggesting that:

> The initial reign of Diabolus is the 1,260 days of the Beast of Revelation 12; the first appearance of Emmanuel is the fifth Monarchy; the decline of Mansoul and the attack by Diabolus are explained by the predicted assault by Gog and Magog; and the return of Emmanuel is the resumption to the Fifth Monarchy until the last judgement. [17]

It is true, of course, that the allegory ends not with the establishment of Jesus' reign on earth but his promise to return and with this injunction from Revelation to Mansoul: Hold fast till I come. The Fifth Monarchist claimed that Jesus' reign would succeed the period of the Commonwealth, but to insist on this political level is to be caught up in an inescapable dilemma. Admittedly, all of the levels of the allegory are complex and are essential parts of the *one* allegory Bunyan wrote. To discover the imaginative ways through which he tells his one story in all its unfolding action is perhaps a greater task of the serious critic than is the probing of the various levels. In his central metaphor, Bunyan defines the nature of man's soul, as I suggested earlier, in terms of two antagonistic powers. To develop the metaphor he uses a variety of imaginative devices. One of the most pervading is contrast.

There is a series of contrasts that stress completeness and beauty before the capture of Mansoul or before man fell as opposed to the disorder and fragmentation brought on by man's disobedience. For example, the builder of Mansoul was Shaddai, and he 'built it for his own delight. He made it the mirror, and glory of all that he made even the top-piece beyond any thing else that he did in that country' (p. 8). The 'town' was so beautiful and perfect that 'it is said, by some, the gods at the setting up thereof, came down to see it, and sang for joy' (p. 8). Further glory and strength characterise Mansoul in that it had always a sufficiency of provision within its walls; it had the best, most wholesome, and excellent law that there was extant in the world. There was not a rascal, rogue, or traitorous person then within its walls: They were all true men, and fast joined together . . . And to all these, it was always (so long as it had the goodness to keep true to Shaddai, the King) his countenance, his protection, and his delight. (p. 9)

But this was the prelapsarian state of Mansoul.

The 'then-now' contrast also underlies the depiction of Diabolus. He was at first 'one of the servants of King Shaddai, made, and taken and put by him into most high and mighty place' (p. 10). But Diabolus was not satisfied, for he 'began to think with himself, how he might be set up as honour over all and have the sole power under Shaddai' (p. 10). This thought eventuates into an action, designed by Diabolus, to take the place reserved solely for Shaddai's son; consequently the 'glory' of Diabolus ends as Shaddai casts him and his cohorts out of 'all places of trust, benefit, honour, and preferment' and turns them down into 'the horrible pit'.

If Bunyan appropriates contrast to show the state of Mansoul and Diabolus before the fall, so similarly does he portray the continual warfare between Shaddai and Diabolus for the soul of man, especially the elect, as well as man's struggle within to live a holy life in an unholy world. Not as a 'great and mighty prince' but 'under the shape and body of a dragon', Diabolus, through subtle arguments, wins his way into the 'castle' which Shaddai built in Mansoul — a castle which, in contrast, now becomes a 'den' and 'hold' for Diabolus.

Bunyan continues to use contrast to show the nature of the imperfect state. Whereas Lord Understanding and Mr Conscience were in prominent places of power when Shaddai reigned over Mansoul, they are replaced by Lord Lustings and Forget-good when Diabolus captures the town. Bunyan sharply draws the contrast in the lives of the two leaders after Diabolus becomes king. Lord Understanding, because he was a 'seeing man', is not allowed to keep his 'former lustre and glory' but rather is 'alienated from the light' and becomes 'as one born blind'. Moreover, Mr Conscience, before the town was taken, was a man 'well read in the laws of his King, and also a man of courage and faithfulness to speak the truth at every occasion' (p. 21). Diabolus 'debauched the man', 'stupefied' his mind, hardened his heart and 'so drew him into sin and wickedness' that he was almost 'past all conscience of sin' (pp. 21–2).

High among the gentry under Shaddai was Lord Willbewill, a man 'of great strength, resolution, and courage, nor in his occasion could any turn him away' (p. 24). But, now Lord Willbewill's mind 'stood bending' towards service to Diabolus, and the latter made him Captain of the Castle, Governor of the Wall, and 'Keeper of the Gates of Mansoul'.

When Diabolus captures Mansoul, Bunyan states that the town was 'wholly at his beck', and brought 'wholly to his bow', and 'nothing was heard or seen therein but that which tended to set up him' (pp. 27-8). After Diabolus' brief reign and when Emmanuel marches into Mansoul, the people, in contrast, now 'cringe, bow, bend', and wish 'a thousand times over' that Emmanuel would become their 'Prince and Captain'.

Contrast or antithesis of phrases, at its loftiest, is the description of the people of Mansoul when Emmanuel grants them pardon:

> . . .they went down to the camp in black, but they came back to the town in white; they went down to the camp in ropes, they came back in chains of gold; they went down to the camp with feet in fetters, but they came back with their steps enlarged under them; they went also to the camp looking for death, but they came back from thence with assurance of life; they went down to the camp with heavy hearts, but came back again with pipes and tabor playing before them. (p. 123)

But when Carnal Security makes his inroads, the people of Mansoul seem to forget the remarkable features of their pardon. In four statements, Bunyan shows the contrast in attitude towards Emmanuel:

1. They left off their former way of visiting of him; they came not to his royal palace as afore.
2. They did not regard, nor yet take notice that he came or came not to visit them.
3. The love-feasts that had wont to be between their Prince and them, though he made them still, and called them to them, yet they neglected to come at them, or to be delighted with them.
4. They wanted not for his counsels, but began to be

headstrong and confident in themselves; concluding that now they were strong and invincible, and that Mansoul was secure, and beyond all reach of the foe, and that her state must needs be unalterable for ever. (pp.173-4)

Contrast is a primary literary means of working out the defining metaphor of *The Holy War*; it is no surprise that Bunyan turns again to this device when the allegory is practically at its end. Emmanuel contrasts the source of the recent struggles and the source of remedy: 'the way of backsliding was thine, but the way and means of thy recovery was mine' (p. 279).

Not only does he show in this last statement contrast between two sources, but Bunyan also asserts a principle which he threads throughout the allegory: the personal responsibility of the individual in the experience of salvation.

In his initial description of Mansoul, for example, he declares that the town walls were built so well that never could they fall except through the deliberate act of the people. When Mansoul repents of its backslidden condition, they urge the Lord Secretary to draw up a petition for them to Prince Emmanuel. At the centre of the negotiations, Bunyan places responsibility on man:

'Well,' said the Lord Secretary, 'I will draw up a petition for you, and will also set my hand thereto.' Then said they, 'But when shall we call for it at the hands of our Lord?' But he answered, 'Yourselves must be present at the doing of it. Yes, you must put your desires to it. True, the hand and pen shall be mine, but the ink and paper must be yours; else how can you say it is your petition? Nor have I need to petition for myself, because I have not offended.' (pp. 235-6)

In matters of grace God takes the initiative, but He will not force His pardon on man; 'the ink and paper' must be man's: co-operation with God's initiative is essential.

The significance which Bunyan attaches to Lord Willbewill not only strikes the note of personal responsibility but assigns man's will to a place of superiority. What Bunyan delineates is that the will is involved whether man serves God or the devil. Captain Boanerges and his army are unable to subdue the Diabolonian forces so long as Lord Willbewill as governor supports the mayor, Lord Lustings, or his successor, Lord Incredulity. But when

Emmanuel rids Mansoul of the enemy and revamps the chaotic administrative posts, Lord Willbewill leaves the Diabolonians and becomes an ardent follower of the new order, and the external forces of Doubters cannot overthrow Mansoul as long as Willbewill works in obedience to Emmanuel and in opposition to the forces of evil.

Skilful handling of character is also noteworthy in Bunyan's story of warfare. James Forrest believes that there is a valuable literary husbandry in his character portrayals, a deft trick of the ancient art of character-writing that was revived in the Renaissance.[18] He refers to that old Diabolonian, Mr Loth-to-Stoop, as 'a stiff man in his way' or of the recognisable human classification of Lord Lustings, 'the son of one Beastly whose mother, the daughter of Evil Concupiscence, bear him in Flesh Street'. Other apt classifications might be added: old Mr Prejudice, who keeps Eargate with 60 deaf men; Mr Anything, who has both sides against him because he is true to none; Hard-heart, who never knew either remorse or sorrow all his life; or Carnal-Security, who stands always, in his way of standing, with what he supposes to be the strongest side.

In Bunyan's treatment of characters, there is a remarkable willingness to do justice to those whose practices are antithetical to his beliefs. Willbewill, for example, becomes an officer under Diabolus so that 'he might be a petty Ruler and Governor in Mansoul', but Bunyan also avers that Willbewill is a man 'of great strength, resolution, and courage'. When Mr Haughty receives his indictment, the court states that he is indicted neither for being a valiant man, nor for having used his strengths to draw the town of Mansoul into acts of rebellion. That Bunyan is able to show balance in his portrayal of some individuals is a tribute to his artistry.[19]

If Bunyan strikingly appropriates contrast to shape aspects of the spiritual warfare, if he insists on personal responsibility in winning the battles of a holy war, and if his handling of character shows masterful control and remarkable fairness, so also does he frequently use parody with special excellence.

A classic example is the speech of Diabolus to the people of Mansoul in which he ironically twists the images of the sixth chapter of Ephesians into his own specially designed armour. Speaking as an inspired leader in an attempt to quiet the fears of the people of Mansoul, who have heard that Shaddai will retake the town, he

declares: 'Armour for you I have and by me it is; Yea, and it is sufficient for Mansoul from top to tow.' His armour consists of
'Helmet, Breast-plate, Sword and Shield . . . that will make you
fight like men!' The helmet protects any who wear it 'from Arrow,
Dart, Sword, Shield'. The breast-plate is of iron and forged in
Diabolus' own country . . . 'and, in plain language, it is an hard
heart, an heart as hard as iron, as much past feeling as a stone. . .'
The sword is a tongue that is 'set on fire of hell' and the shield is
unbelief 'calling into question . . . all the sayings of Shaddai'. A
final part of the armour is 'a dumb and prayerless Spirit, a spirit
that scorns to cry for mercy' (pp. 38-9). A superb piece of self-
characterisation is this parody;[20] the self-assurance and glee of the
speaker mark well not only his view of his own ability but also
clearly delineate the deception and arrogance of Emmanuel's
enemy.

Another excellent example of parody is the one on the colour
symbolism and the emblems of the 'scutcheons' of Prince
Emmanuel's captains. The captains bear the traditional colours:
Captain Charity, green for youth; Captain Innocent, white for
purity or innocence; Captain Patience, black for suffering. The
scutcheon of Captain Credence is the holy lamb and golden
shield, the lamb of God and the shield of faith; the scutcheon of
Captain Goodhope is three golden anchors or the three-fold
anchor of Hebrews 6:19; the scutcheon of Captain Charity is three
naked orphans embraced in the bosom[21] or the supremacy of love;
the scutcheon of Captain Innocent is three golden doves or harmless-
ness; and the scutcheon of Captain Patience is three arrows
through the golden heart of longsuffering.

Rather than five captains, Diabolus has nine with names like
Captain Rage, Captain Fury, Captain Damnation, Captain
Torment, and others of a similarly destructive nature. The colour
symbolism is either red (but not in the traditional sense) or pale for
each captain, and the scutcheons include such horrendous figures
as 'black den', 'yawning jaws', 'the ghastly picture of death', and 'a
skull, and dead men's bones'. The entire catalogue of captains, forces, ancients, colours, and scutcheons constitutes a parody of
Prince Emmanuel's hosts; the device permits Bunyan to show not
only the nature of the enemy that wars against man but also that
the demonic world is diametrically opposed to the infinitely
glorious state for which man battles.

Numerous images serve a purpose similar to the parodies.

When Mansoul prepares for the reception of Prince Emmanuel after he delivers them from Diabolus, Bunyan speaks of the preparation in images of renewal such as 'green trees', 'meadows', 'boughs and flowers', and'garlands'. Far different are the images associated with the sad state of Mansoul, when Diabolus and his army invade a second time; for images of disintegration abound: 'now did Mansoul seem to be nothing but a den of dragons, an emblem of Hell, and a place of total darkness. Now did Mansoul lie almost like the barren wilderness; nothing but nettles, briars, thorns, weeds, and stinking things seemed now to cover the face of Mansoul' (p. 232).

To show the joy that belongs to Emmanuel and his followers, Bunyan selects on occasion the image of harmonious music. At times the music is so melodious that those that 'dwell in the highest orbs' would open their windows in wonder. From the followers of Diabolus, there blares forth the discordant, hideous 'roaring of the drum'. Music becomes, in Bunyan's hands, a magnificent imaginative statement on the polarity of the two warring forces.

Another arresting characteristic of Bunyan's art is the sheer beauty of language. Perhaps few sections are equal to the description of the people of Mansoul when they hear their pardon read: 'but who can think what a turn, what a change, what an alteration . . . joy and music . . . telling and hearing' (p. 124). Just as beautifully and aptly handled is the striking balance of sentences. Immediately following exclamations over the 'agility, nimbleness, dexterity, and bravery' of Prince Emmanuel's army, Bunyan writes an excellent demonstration of balance and counterbalance:

> They marched, they counter-marched; they opened to the right and left; they divided and subdivided; they closed, they wheeled; made good their front and rear with their right and left wings . . . But add to this, the handling of their arms, the managing of their weapons of war, were marvelous taking to Mansoul and me. (p. 126)

Homely, idiomatic expressions, though prevalent, are less abundant in *The Holy War* than in many writings of Bunyan. One of the finest epigrammatic statements is the one he gives to the forces of Diabolus. To underscore the plotting of the enemy, they say: 'When people are most busy in the world, they least fear a surprise' (pp.191-2).

Examples of anaphora point to another feature of Bunyan's imaginative telling of his allegory. When the inhabitants of Mansoul begin to see their folly in sinning against Emmanuel, they remorsefully say in their third petition to the Prince: 'If thou wilt slay us, we have deserved it. If thou wilt condemn us to the deep, we cannot but say thou art righteous' (p. 112). Before this petition, in the statement from the famous parody on Paul's statements to the Ephesians to put on the whole armour of God, Diabolus asserts: 'If he speaks of judgment, care not for it; if he speaks of mercy, care not for it; if he promises, if he swears that he would do to Mansoul . . . regard not what is said . . . ' (p. 39).

Bunyan's dialogue is frequently as alive and telling as in excellent passages of *The Pilgrim's Progress*. When Mr Carnal Security tricks Mr Godlyfear into attending a feast for Mansoul, all of the guests, with the exception of Mr Godlyfear, are eating and drinking and having a carousing time, but Mr Godlyfear, participating in none of the merriment, sits 'like a stranger'. Mr Carnal Security, perceiving his unhappiness, says:

> Carn. Mr. Godlyfear, are you not well? You seem to be ill of body or mind, or both. I have a cordial of Mr. Forget-good's making, the which, sir, if you will take a dram of, I hope it may make you bonny and blithe, and so make you fit for we feasting companions.
> Godly. . . . Sir, I thank you for all things courteous and civil, but for your cordial I have no list thereto . . . to me it is strange to see you so jocund and merry, when the town of Mansoul is in such woeful case. (p. 175-6)

The dialogue has a degree of concrete particularity, it vividly contrasts the two characters, and it gives the flavour of colloquial speech. Undoubtedly, one of the peculiar powers of Bunyan's style is the way in which he can maintain a colloquial mode of speaking, even while dealing with large theological doctrines. In the episode dealing with the intrusion of various Doubters into the town of Mansoul, he discusses issues of Election, Vocation or Calling, Salvation and Grace, not in the language of Systematic Theology, but in 'market town' terminology. One illustration will suffice:

But there were three of those that came from the land of Doubting,

who after they had wond'red and ranged the country a while, and
perceived that they had escaped, were so hardy as to thrust
themselves, knowing that yet there were in the town Diabolonians. Three, did I say? I think there were four. Now to whose
house should these Diabolonian Doubters go, but to the house
of an old Diabolonian in Mansoul, whose name was Evil-
questioning; a very great enemy he was to Mansoul, and a great
doer among the Diabolonians there. Well, to this Evil-
questioning's house, as was said, did these Diabolonians come
. . . so he made them welcome, pitied their misfortune, and suc-
coured them with the best that he had in his house. Now after a
little acquaintance (and it was not long before they had that),
this old Evil-questioning asked the Doubters if they were all of a
town . . . and they answered, *No, nor not of one shire, neither*, 'For
I,' said one, 'am an Election-doubter.' 'I,' said another, 'am a
Vocation-doubter.' Then said the third, 'I am a Salvation-
doubter,' and the fourth said he was a Grace-doubter. 'Well,'
quoth the old gentleman, 'be of what shire you will, I am persuaded that you are down boys: you have the very length of my
foot, are one with my heart, and shall be welcome to me.' So they
thanked him, and were glad that they had found themselves an
harbour in Mansoul. (pp. 266-7)

Interrupting questions, interspersed dialogue, and the amiable
tone of this colloquial mode of narration give an immediacy to
abstract theological terms.

As long and sustained as *The Holy War* is, it is not without the
sudden turns and unexpected developments, frequently found in
The Pilgrim's Progress. Bunyan introduces Carnal Security, for
example, when Mansoul's happiness seems unable to reach
greater heights, but Bunyan firmly believes that at the moment
when one least expects, the enemy makes his inroads. The force of
the sudden turn is enormously strengthened by the calm manner
in which Bunyan introduces Carnal Security. After receiving pardon from Emmanuel, the whole town of Mansoul enjoys
unparalleled happiness, and 'nothing was to be found but harmony, quietness, joy and health. And this lasted all that summer'
(p. 170). Suddenly, without the slightest hint that this triumphant
note will terminate. Bunyan simply says, 'But there was a man
in the town of Mansoul, and his name was Mr. Carnal Security;
this man did, after all this mercy bestowed on this corporation,

bring the Town of Mansoul into great and grievous slavery and bondage' (p. 170).

Not all the separate features would convince us, however, of the quality of Bunyan's art were they not fused into an organic whole. Various kinds of contrast, 'character-writing', parody, imagery, idiomatic expression, lively dialogue, and sheer beauty of language reinforce each other to tell Bunyan's story of man's constant warfare.

One other literary device, perhaps Bunyan's favourite, the riddle, must be observed. Near the end of 'An Advertisement to the Reader', he suggests that the entire work is a riddle, only to be resolved through his 'window' or his key. As if to illustrate the earnestness of his statement he concludes with an anagram of his name: 'Witness my name, if anagram'd to thee / The letters make, *Nu hony in a B.*' The anagram refers, of course, to Samson's riddle of the bees and the honey in the carcass of a lion. In the allegory proper, Bunyan turns again to the story of Samson when he refers to the scutcheon of Captain Experience as 'the dead lion, and dead bear.' (p. 155). At another stage of the spiritual warfare, when the captain hears Mr Prywell's report, Bunyan says of them: '. . . they being always true lovers of the town of Mansoul, what do they but like so many Samsons they shake themselves, and come together to consult and contrive how to defeat those bold and hellish contrivances . . .' (p. 207-8).

The power of the riddle, and indeed to some extent, the power of imaginative literature, is to open one's eyes to something new and true. Following the feast, celebrating the recovery of Mansoul by Emmanuel, the Prince entertains the people with riddles and expounds some to them. Here is the reaction to the riddles:

> . . . but oh! how they were light'ned! They saw what they never saw; they could not have thought that such rarities could have been couched in so few and such ordinary words. I told you before whom these riddles did concern; and as they were opened, the people did evidently see 'twas so. Yea, they did gather that the things themselves were a kind of a portraiture, and that of Emmanuel himself; for when they read in the scheme where the riddles were writ, and looked in the face of the Prince, things looked so like the one to the other, that Mansoul could not forbear but say, '*This is the Lamb!* This is the *Sacrifice*! This is the *Rock* . . . And this is the *Way*! — with a great many other things more. (pp. 132-3)[22]

The riddle becomes for the people of Mansoul something significant. It is not a mere embellishment for them; it sparks their imaginations and minds to discover new insights. Words with which the people are familiar, when combined in new ways, are capable not simply of illustrating meaning, but of creating it.

Not only did the riddle, in its particularity, point to new and extended meanings, but the long, and perhaps overloaded allegory, *The Holy War,* is a riddle that reveals a new setting for the familiar warfare in human life. When this 'riddling' power is even partially accepted, perhaps readers will come slightly closer to Forrest's belief that *The Holy War* has a 'mythic power' that goes beyond sectarian interests.[23]

Notes

1. Roger Sharrock, *John Bunyan* (London, 1954), p. 136.
2. Lord Macaulay, *The Miscellaneous Writings and Speeches* (London, 1871), p. 359.
3. John Tulloch, *English Puritanism and its Leaders* (London, 1861), p. 472.
4. G.B. Harrison, *John Bunyan: A Study in Personality* (New York, 1928), pp. 198-9.
5. C.S. Lewis, *Allegory of Love* (New York, 1958), p. 69.
6. Ibid.
7. 'Introduction', *The Holy War* (New York, 1967), p. x.
8. Ibid, p. xiii.
9. Sharrock, *John Bunyan*, p. 121.
10. C. Baird, *John Bunyan, A Study in Narrative Technique* (Port Washington, NY, 1977), p. 37.
11. I. MacCaffrey, *Spenser's Allegory* (Princeton, 1976), p. 37.
12. Ibid., p. 38.
13. *John Bunyan,* Courtenay Studies in Reformation Theology (Grand Rapids, 1969), p. 50.
14. 'Introduction', *The Holy War*, p. xv.
15. 'Bunyan's *Holy War*', *Theology Today*, *3* (1946-7), p. 461.
16. W.Y. Tindall, *John Bunyan, Mechanick Preacher* (New York, 1934), p. 157.
17. Ibid., pp. 156-7.
18. 'Introduction', *The Holy War*, p. xvi.
19. Cf. Lynn Veach Sadler, *John Bunyan* (Boston, 1979), pp. 85-7, for provocative insights on Bunyan's treatment of character.
20. See Forrest, ed, *The Holy War*, p. 40, n. 28 for comments on the power of this parody.
21. I share James Forrest's belief that the third scutcheon is a little more mysterious than the other four and that there is a probability that Bunyan here shows his awareness of the representation of Charity in medieval and Renaissance iconography as a mother-figure surrounded by infants (see Forrest, ibid., p. 78, n. 4). It is of some interest also to note that of all the scutcheons, the third is the only one that does not include the word golden; admittedly, if the word were included, the scutcheon might be even more mysterious.
22. All quotations are reprinted by permission of New York University Press and the Copp Clark Publishing Company from James F. Forrest (ed.), *The Holy War.* Copyright 1967 by the Copp Clark Publishing Company.
23. Forrest, ibid., p. xviii.

6 *EMBLEMS*

Emblematic passages in Bunyan's allegories, particularly in *The Pilgrim's Progress*, underscore and enlarge the allegorical effects of both parts. To a lesser extent are there emblems in *The Holy War*, in fact, the 'emblematic' features of formal descriptions, like the escutcheons, usually explained by marginal references, are as close as Bunyan usually comes to the emblem. What becomes evident in a study of his emblems is that he obviously finds fertile soil from which to handle 'Figure' and 'Similitude' in this popular Renaissance phenomenon, the Emblem. So popular was this form that over 600 writers produced over 2,000 emblem books during the sixteenth and seventeenth centuries.

Since the emblem tradition has already received careful and scholarly study,[1] it is wise to limit discussion of its history to a few statements. The first published and circulated emblem book was Andrea Alciati's *Emblematum Liber*, printed by Henry Steyner at Augsburg in 1530. Influential on the form the emblem took, the *Emblematum Liber* was also an exceedingly popular book, which according to Henry Green, went through 175 editions throughout Europe and in England by 1750.[2] The first English collection of emblems[3] was Geoffrey Whitney's. *A Choice of Emblems*, published in 1586. Other writers associated with emblems were Henry Peacham, George Wither, Christopher Harvey, John Hall, John Barber, Francis Quarles and others; the significance of the emblematic habit of mind was also notable in the poetry of Spenser, Herbert, and Crashaw.

In its strictest sense, the Emblem consists of a picture illustrating some moral truth followed by a scriptural citation, a poem commenting on the significance of the picture, a quotation, or quotations, from the Church Fathers or other authorities, and frequently a concluding epigram. Bargali, an Italian exponent of the science of emblem writing declared that the words and the pictures were to be 'so strictly united together, that being considered apart, they cannot explicate themselves distinctly the one without the other'.[4] No doubt Bargali was primarily interested in guaranteeing that readers not overlook the 'meaning' of the visual, but his precautions suggest the picture as an essential component of emblem writing. The emblematic habit of mind, however, pervaded the writings of various English writers,[5] who certainly felt no compulsion to follow Bargali's strictures. Absent from Bunyan's writings, not specifically categorised as Emblems, but with emblematic figures and episodes, is the picture. *Divine Emblems,* formerly titled *Country Rhymes for Boys and Girls,* appeared in the original without pictures, plates or woodcuts.[6]

The implicit presence of the picture, not the picture itself, is essential in emblematic writing. The emblem belongs, as does other 'literary' writing, to the kind which Northrop Frye in his *Anatomy of Criticism* calls an autonomous verbal structure, or writing in which the final direction of meaning resides in our perception[7] and this direction comes through symbolic 'literary' language — whether simile, metaphor, personification, or other rhetorical devices. Furthermore, as D.W. Robertson Jr. says, 'the delight in the enigmatic which appears in . . . musical configurations of the fourteenth century, and in the emblem books of the Renaissance is not something merely "quaint" . . . the enigmatic figure was one of the most powerful and effective instruments by means of which the . . . artist could fulfil the aims of his art'.[8] The emblem and other enigmatic figures enable the writer 'to appeal, first of all, to the reason, and through the reason to the affective values which philosophy and theology pointed to as the highest and most moving values possible to humanity'.[9] What we expect then is the 'talking-picture' of the literary description and the 'picture of signification or transformation into moral meaning'.[10]

Obviously, a strong didactic quality is implicit in this form of figurative expression, especially in Bunyan's *Emblems*, but it is easy to mistake the surface application for 'crudity' and artistic ineptitude.[11] It is essential not to ignore the emblematist's belief that configuration of known things or objects stimulates perception of an underlying truth and order.[12] As Peter Daly succinctly states, both 'the medieval allegorist and the renaissance emblematist held that everything that exists points to meanings beyond the things themselves'. He also holds that the 'relationship of meanings to created thing is not arbitrary or capricious in this world view' even though 'a single object like the sun could be seen from twenty different points of view, connoting twenty different meanings'.[13]

That Bunyan knew how to take 'known things' and stimulate 'perception of an underlying truth and order' or that he knew how to direct the reader from the concrete materials of the figures to something underneath the language or beyond the figure is evident in his writings. Furthermore, in various works he refers to his theoretical belief in using concrete and known objects to lead the mind toward a perception of something invisible.

In *Solomon's Temple Spiritualized* (1688), for example, Bunyan writes: 'Since it is the wisdom of God to speak to us oft time by trees, gold, silver, stones, beasts, fowls, fishes, spiders, ants, frogs, flies, lice, dust, etc., and here by wood; how should we by them understand his voice if we count there is no meaning in them?'[14]

Bunyan's stance is similar to what Emile Mâle asserts about the thoughtful man of the Middle Ages: 'The world is a symbol, "an idea of God made manifest in the Word" . . . the world is a great book written by the hand of God, in which every being is a word charged with meaning.'[15] Certainly, Christian thinkers from the time of Augustine stressed how significant is the knowledge of the characteristic nature of things or animals named in Scripture. Augustine himself says:

> . . . an imperfect knowledge of things causes figurative passages to be obscure; for example, when we do not recognize the nature of the animals, minerals, plants, or other things which are very often represented in Scripture for the sake of an analogy. It is well known that a serpent exposes its whole body, rather than its head, to those attacking it, and how clearly that explains the Lord's meaning when he directed us to be 'wise as serpents'. We should, therefore, expose our body to persecutors, rather than our head, which is Christ. Thus, the Christian faith, the head so to speak, may not be killed in us, as it would be if, preserving our body, we were to reject God! . . . A knowledge of the nature of the serpent, therefore, explains many analogies which Holy Scripture habitually makes from that animal; so a lack of knowledge about other animals to which Scripture no less frequently alludes for comparison hinders a reader very much. The same is true of an ignorance of minerals and plants . . . knowledge of the carbuncle . . . also illumines many obscure passages . . . and an ignorance of the beryl or the diamond frequently closes the door to understanding.[16]

What Bunyan does in his emblems is, as Augustine suggests, to think in analogies. In the view of Augustine, Bunyan, and other medieval and renaissance writers, God endowed the world, the book of nature, with meaning, which all should seek to understand, as well as to discover in it new meanings.

I have already referred to Bunyan's practice of the emblematic attitude in *The Pilgrim's Progress*. Perhaps one of the most famous examples is in the first part of *The Pilgrim's Progress,* an episode with people, objects and action, and one that Sharrock calls 'an emblem theatre'.[17] In each room, visual scenes appear before Christian and the Interpreter explains and applies their meaning. There are: the dusty room which a girl sprinkles with water before a man with a broom brushes it clean; the room with the two children, Patience and Passion; the room in which a man seeks to extinguish with water a fire burning against a wall, secretly fed with oil by a hand behind the wall; and the dark room containing a man in an iron cage. Other scenes include the man with the muck rake, the spider that lives in a beautiful room, the garden where all the flowers grow and live in harmony, and the fair-appearing tree, rotten at the heart.

What David Alpaugh sees in these emblems within emblems goes beyond what Christian sees, for he says 'the art of emblem interpretation that Christian learns, as the Interpreter explains the significance of a number of emblems by the light of Illumination, is in a larger sense the art that all aspiring pilgrims must learn before they can enter the Celestial City'.[18] Other emblematic episodes, hardly on the scale of that of the Interpreter's House, are scattered through *The Pilgrim's Progress.*

In the Valley of the Shadow of Death, Christian confronts dangers upon dangers: 'Snares, Traps, Gins . . . Nets . . . Pits, Pitfalls, deep holes'. But simultaneously, Bunyan speaks of 'the Sun rising', then reiterates, 'as I said, just now the Sun was rising' and then gives to Christian the words: 'His candle shineth on my head, and by his light I go through darkness.' The candle, the rising Sun, the light are 'the known objects' which point towards the light of Christ's presence. Another emblematic episode is evident when Christian and Hopeful come upon a strange thing, a monument, which looks as though it had been a woman transformed into a pillar. After Hopeful points to an inscription on the pillar, Christian puts together the meaning, 'Remember Lot's wife.' The two pilgrims talk at length upon what the event entails, and how it applies to their lives.

In the second part of *The Pilgrim's Progress* there is a 'theatre' of emblems both inside and outside the Interpreter's house. The Interpreter shows Christiana and her fellow-pilgrims 'what Christian, Christiana's husband had seen sometime before', but he also shows new emblems to the new pilgrims. For their understanding and growth, the Interpreter shows them the celebrated figure, the man with the muck rake, which Roger Sharrock calls 'emblematic to the finger-tips' and the 'most effective' of all Bunyan's collections of emblems.[19] In an extended point by point explanation of the visual details, the Interpreter leads the mind of Christiana and her 'Company' from the things visible to new meanings. Note the emblem:

> ... the *Interpreter* takes them apart again: and has them first into a Room, *where was a man that could look no way but downwards, with a Muckrake in his hand. There stood also one over his head with a Celestial Crown in his Hand, and proffered to give him the Crown for the Muck-rake; but the man did neither look up, nor regard; but raked to himself the Straws, the small Sticks, and Dust of the Floor.*[20]

After Christiana sees the figure, the dialogue continues with the following interchange:

> Then said *Christiana, I perswade my self that I know somewhat the meaning of this: For this is a Figure of a man of this world: Is it not, good Sir?* Inter. Thou has said the right, said he, and his *Muck-rake* doth show his Carnal Mind. And whereas thou seest him rather give heed to rake up Straws and Sticks, and the Dust of the Floor, than to what he says that calls to him from above with the Celestial Crown in his Hand; it is to show, That Heaven is but a Fable to some, and that things here are counted the only things substantial. Now whereas it was also showed thee, that the man could look no way but downwards: It is to let thee know that earthly things when they are with Power upon Mens minds, quite carry their hearts away from God. Chrs. *Then said* Christiana, O! deliver me from *this Muck-rake.*
> Inter. That Prayer said the *Interpreter*, has lain by till 'tis almost rusty: *Give me NOT Riches*, is scarce the Prayer of one of ten thousand, Straws, and Sticks, and Dust, with most, are the great things now looked after.[21]

Not only is the tableau vivid: a man looking downward, a muck rake, straws, sticks, dust, and One above offering a celestial crown for the muck rake, but the picture is an excellent portraiture of Bunyan's emblematic writing in that the concrete objects are components of a 'Figure' which points towards the invisible.

But there are other emblems for Christiana to view: the spider, dwelling in the 'best room' of the house; the hen and chickens, compared to 'the King' and his 'Obedient ones'; the butcher and the sheep in the slaughter house, suggesting the patience with which one suffers; the flowers in the field, all as the 'gardiner had set them', connoting the diversities of Christians with each in his proper place; the bad crops — telling again that fruitlessness is condemned 'to the Fire'; the 'little Robbin with a great Spider in his mouth'; pointing to the difference between appearance and reality; and the tree, rotten at the heart, whose 'out-side is fair' but whose 'inside is rotten'. Before beginning her journey through the Valley of the Shadow of Death, Christiana is given the Golden Anchor that hung on a wall in the Palace Beautiful in case she meets with turbulent weather. The anchor which she receives is an emblem signifying hope that, as Daly states, 'only by a considerable stretch of the imagination, may preserve her on land against the physical storms of the Valley; it will certainly provide her with spiritual strength to withstand the fear of death'.[22]

No doubt these rich and varied emblems on commonplace subjects are almost special pleas from Bunyan that the distance between the visible and invisible not go unobserved; or, as Sharrock aptly states, 'these emblem passages ... are a reminder to the casual reader that he will only draw the full content of meaning if he is continually looking behind the story to the parable and the occult reference ...' [23] Furthermore, as James F. Forrest perceptively shows (in his discussion of Mercy's yearning for the looking-glass in the second part of *The Pilgrim's Progress*), Bunyan does far more than simply give a counterpart to an incident of Part One in which the Shepherd lends Christian and Hopeful the 'perspective glass'. Not only does Bunyan adopt the scriptural use of the looking-glass as a metaphor of God's Word and as a reflector of mental content, but also through the episode he communicates an artistic self-consciousness and acknowledges the comprehension of art as a device through which the sinner is brought face to face with the iniquity of his own mind and taught to see himself as he is.[24] In brief, the surface figure of the action and the inner landscape are always intertwined.

If the emblem pervades *The Pilgrim's Progress*, it is surely less prevalent in *The Holy War* and contributes less to the emotive power of the narrative than in both parts of *The Pilgrim's Progress*. Mansoul itself, in its backslidden predicament, is called an 'emblem of Hell'. The speaking pictures on escutcheons are, as mentioned earlier, the most vivid examples of emblems. Captain Good-Hope's escutcheon has 'Three Golden Anchors', and the allusion gives the source of the anchor as an emblem of hope — Hebrews 6:19: 'This hope we have as an anchor of the soul, a hope both sure and steadfast and one which enters within the Veil.' On Captain Torment's escutcheon is the 'black worm', a reference to Hell, 'where their worm dieth not', a refrain from Mark 9:44, 46, 48.

It is clear, then, that *The Pilgrim's Progress* (Parts One and Two) abounds in emblems, but it is *A Book for Boys and Girls*, or *Country Rhymes for Children*, later called *Divine Emblems*, that contains Bunyan's concentrated effort in emblem writing, a collection of works that he intends as the Preface suggests, for all spiritual children. For to Bunyan, the 'proper subjects' are the 'Boys and Girls of all Sorts and Degrees', and the 'Toys', a term he uses six times in the Preface, and 'playthings' that 'their souls entangle'.

The range of Bunyan's emblematic subjects includes the sacraments or doctrinal and theological topics; other emblems call attention to the transience of temporal things and the brevity of life. The first emblem is a metrical version of the Ten Commandments. His fourth is a metrical version of the Lord's Prayer, the tenth is on the Creed, and the fourteenth is on the two sacraments that Bunyan believes essential for the Christian — baptism and the Eucharist. As these subjects suggest, in disentangling 'boys and girls' from their 'toys', Bunyan no doubt wants religious education to grow from a biblical basis.

Numerous creatures and objects that one would easily observe in the country are those on which Bunyan bases most of his emblematic writing: the bee, an egg, the lark, the spider, the snail, the mole, the cackling of a hen, flint in water, the rose bush, bells, lanterns and others. Rarely does he use abstractions for subjects, but included among these infrequent emblems are 'Of Beauty', 'Upon Time and Eternity', 'Of Physick', 'Of Man by Nature', and 'Upon Death'. Several focus on the vanity of wordly things, a motif strong in Bunyan's Vanity Fair. The mole (XIX), the butterfly

(XXI), the frog (XXXVI), and the boy with his plums (XLVII) are typical. Absent from Bunyan's emblems are the two images which R.J. Clements declares are the most popular among Renaissance emblematists — the laurel and the swan.[25] Conspicuously absent, too, are floral images, particularly the rose and the lily, with their specialised connotations of virginity, profane love, and mortality.[26] Not even the 'obsequious marigold', which to George Wither suggests multiplied resemblances between the flower's conduct before the sun and man's conduct before God, is among Bunyan's images.

Rarely does Bunyan look to music for his emblems, a surprise when we remember his love for music. In 'Of the Child at the Bush' (Emblem XXXI), the child (Christ) entices the bird (the sinner) with the 'unthought-of-music' of heaven. 'Upon a Ring of Bells' (Emblem XXIX) suggests the captivating power of well-rung bells and then shows the bells as analogous to the human being: the bells are the powers of the soul; the clappers, the passions; the steeple, the body. 'Upon a Skilful Player on an Instrument' (LIX) discloses the power of music to appeal to the ear, mind, and spirit. Following the frequent pattern, the comparison views the image as an emblem of the 'Gospel-minister' who skilfully handles every word, whether he preaches of wrath or of grace.

One of his most aesthetically satisfying emblems is on the sun, a subject he uses several times. 'Upon the Sun's Reflection on the Clouds in a Fair Morning' (Emblem XV), compares the prayers of saints to 'smoky curdled clouds'. The fowler image, which Bunyan describes in the preface to *The Pilgrim's Progress,* Part One, as one of his own artistic methods, becomes an emblem for the Devil in Upon the Lark and the Fowler' (Emblem XXIII), and in 'Upon Our Being Afraid of the Apparition of Evil Spirits' (Emblem LXV).

Whatever Bunyan chooses as his subject he usually adapts it to his own purposes and never wearies of explaining its significance. His usual format is to describe an object in several lines and then draw a comparison. Temporal things *are* 'spiritualized', and Bunyan's primary interest is not with an emblematic tradition or with poetic glory, but rather with 'talking-pictures' of objects he knew best as means of pointing towards intangible qualities that he believed man needed most. This is not necessarily to be considered a weakness, for as Rosemary Freeman aptly states, Bunyan's handling of the convention is, in fact, much freer than that of his predecessors; he has not collected his material from familiar literary sources nor is he tied to a particular mode of representation. The "emblematic" quality of his images depends not upon their content but only upon their application.'[27]

His treatment of time, however, is by no means dissimilar to the handling of the subject by numerous writers. Erwin Panofsky in referring to time as a 'Revealer' and as a 'Destroyer' states concerning the latter that 'it was from the image of Time that, about the last years of the fifteenth century, the representations of Death began to borrow the hourglass'.[28] Undoubtedly, Bunyan's classic example of Time as destroyer is his emblem, 'Upon an Hour-Glass', for 'Time more, nor less' by the glass 'will out be spun'. Focusing more pointedly on the destructive power of time, he concludes the emblem with this comparison:

Man's Life, we will compare unto this Glass
The number of his Months he cannot pass;
But when he has accomplished his day
He, like a Vapour, vanisheth away. (p. 61)

But in sharp contrast are Bunyan and Whitney, for example, in their treatment of the subject, the bee. Whitney's emblem has a woodcut depicting a hive with returning insects; the title under the picture is 'Patria cuique chara'. Not only does the 'maister bee' rule mercifully and orderly, but the other bees are patriotic, loyal, and diligent and 'all the days the honie home doe beare'.[29] Bunyan's handling is far different:

'Upon the Bee'

The Bee goes out and Honey home doth bring;
And some who seek that Honey find a sting
Now woulds't thou have the Honey and be free
From stinging; in the first place kill the Bee.

Comparison

This Bee an Emblem truly is of sin
Whose Sweet unto a many death hath been.
Now woulds't have Sweet from sin, and yet not dye?
Do thou it in the first place mortifie. (p. 11)[30]

If he differs from other emblematists in his 'moralisations' of the implied picture, Bunyan is just as likely to show various inconsistencies within his own emblems. Whitney, for example, holds to the traditional meaning of the symbolism of insects drawn toward the flame of a candle: admonition against profane love. But, in 'Of the Fly at the Candle', Bunyan states:

> This Candle is an Emblem of that Light
> Our Gospels gives in this our darksome Night:
> The Fly a lively picture is of those
> That hate and do this Gospel Light oppose. (p. 29-30)

In 'Meditations upon the Candle' he varies his emblematic object further and shows, with considerable compactness, more than 20 point by point comparisons between a candle and man's spiritual state. The choice of image and comparison is of no serious consequence to Bunyan; in fact, he states his personal concern in his emblem, 'Of the Boy and the Butter-fly':

> The Butter-fly doth represent to me,
> The world's best things at best but fading be. (p. 28)

What may appear to be a narrow or prejudiced way of looking at a creature in the natural world is actually an expression of the emblematist's view of nature. It is a recognition, as J. Paul Hunter says of the emblematic orientation of Defoe, that the physical world is 'a series of emblems . . . made by God to clarify to men great spiritual truths . . .'[31]

If there is a diversity in the emblematic significance of the selected subjects, similarly there is variation in the emblematic structure. At times Bunyan uses dialogue as in 'The Sinner and the Spider'; on other occasions he meshes image and comparison as in the eight-line piece, 'Upon an Hour-Glass'. In 'Upon the Barren Fig Tree in God's Vineyard', through the image of 'barren', Bunyan catalogues in 24 lines the dangers of fruitlessness, and in each fourth line sounds the refrain: 'Bear fruit, or else thy end will cursed be.' Although the emblem has its subject, the fruitless Christian, Bunyan shows, on the other hand, an image of God who is merciful, just, patient, as well as One who can grieve or 'recoil'. But the most frequent pattern is a twofold division: the first part contains the image or the description of the chosen subject; the second section, labelled 'comparison' points the moral. His dialogue deserves more concentrated attention.

In 'The Sinner and the Spider', the work begins with a brief encounter between the two 'characters', then shows the sinner's antipathy for the 'filthy creature', but develops to a reversed position in which the sinner considers himself 'a Fool' and calls the spider his 'Monitor'.

Following the sinner's high claim that he is a man and 'in God's image made', the Spider replies with an admission of man's greatness as a Creature far above a spider, but then retorts:

> But though thy God hath made thee such a Creature,
> Thou hast against him often played the traitor.
>
> . . .
>
> Thy soul, thy Reason, yea thy spotless State,
> Sin has subjected to the most dreadful fate.
> But I have retained my primitive condition,
> I've all, but what I lost by thy Ambition. (p. 19)

Like Henry Vaughan, who sees birds, bees, and flowers ever cleaving to God's 'divine appointments' but also sees man as the one who 'drew the curse upon the world, and cracked / the whole frame with his fall', Bunyan's dialogue has the spider show, too, that it is man, not the creatures, who has departed from his originally appointed place and lost his 'primitive condition'.

To emphasise further the extent of man's sin, the spider makes these spirited comments:

> Hark then; tho man is noble by creation,
> He's lapsed now to such Degeneration;
> Is so besotted, and so careless grown,
> As not to grieve, though he has overthrown
> Himself, and brought to Bondage every thing
> Created, from the Spider to the King.
> Tread not upon me, neither from one go;
> 'Tis man which has brought all the world to No. (pp. 20-1)

But there is a mystery about the spider of such import that man can study the 'riddle' of the spider and know his own destiny, for says the Spider:

Thus in my Ways, God Wisdom doth conceal;
And by my Ways, that Wisdom doth reveal. (p. 23)

By building its web in dark places, the spider shows how 'many
sin with brazen faces, by building in high places' and by entangling
flies in its web, the spider reveals the multiple, ensnaring techni-
ques of the devil to keep man from salvation; on the other hand,
the unabashed persistence of this character, by which it 'can
possess / The Palace of a King', may equally be a paradigm for
man in his pursuit of heaven. The Spider declares to the sinner
both its nature and its meaning:

I seize a Palace, do with hands take hold
Of Doors, of locks, or bolts; yea I am bold. . .
    Yea, if I please I do the highest Stories
ascend, there fit, and so behold the Glories
My self is compos't with, as if I were
One of the chiefest Courtiers that be there.
    Here Lords and Ladies do come round about me,
With grave Demeanour: Nor do any flout me,
For this my brave Adventure, no not they;
They come, they go, but leave me there to stay.
    Now, my Reproacher, I do by all this
Shew how thou may'st possess thy self of Bliss.
Thou art worse than a Spider, but take hold
On Christ the Door, thou shalt not be controul'd
By Him do thou the Heavenly Palace enter,
None chide thee will for this thy brave Adventure.

Through dialogue, Bunyan contrasts man's original state with
his fallen condition and man with an inferior creature, thus creating an emblem that permits a commonplace creature, a spider, to
instruct man.

Emblem LIII, 'Of Fowls Flying in the Air', is an excellent example
of the structure Bunyan's Emblems usually take. With its description and comparison it shows the harmony in the diversity of
man's gifts:

Methinks I see a Sight most excellent,
All Sorts of Birds fly in the Firmament:
Some great, some small, all of a divers kind,

Mine Eye affecting, pleasant to my mind . . .

Comparison

These Birds are Emblems of those men, that shall
Ere long possess the Heaven, their All in All.
   They are each of divers shape, and kind;
To teach, we of all nations there shall find,
   They are some great, some little, as we see;
To show, some great, some small, in Glory be,
   Their flying diversely, as we behold;
Do shew Saints Joys will there be manifold.
   Some glide, some flutter, and some do,
In a mixt way of flying, glory too . . . (p. 52)

Whatever the subject or the structure, Bunyan's concern is primarily not with investing the image or emblem with the entire meaning of the poem, but rather with showing analogies between the image and its spiritual significance. In all he wishes to direct the focus from the physical object or 'temporal thing' to the larger significance of those objects as symbolic of a Reality not limited by time and space. He is able to present the mind and the imagination with an image and a succession of analogies, direct the mind towards similitudes based on corporal things, and thence refer to those spiritual truths contained in the similitudes. For Bunyan, as for many of his age, all things are charged with significant meaning and he attempts to show the intensity of that meaning. That some of his rhymes show poetic *naïveté* no one could deny; that others suggest a spontaneity and vigour is equally true. To Bunyan, the Emblem is another literary form through which he may attack the accusation 'Metaphors make us blind' and declare of the wise, discerning individual:

   . . . he rather stoops,
And seeks to find out what by pins and loops,
By Calves, and Sheep; by Heifers, and by Rams;
By Birds and Herbs, and by the blood of Lambs;
God speaketh to him: And happy is he
That finds the light, and grace that in them be.[32]

100   Emblems

Notes

1. Three studies of exceptional merit are Peter M. Daly, *Literature in the Light of the Emblem* (Toronto, 1979), Roger Sharrock, 'Bunyan and the English Emblem Writers', *The Review of English Studies* (XII, No. 82), 1945, and Rosemary Freeman, *English Emblem Books* (London, 1945). Daly shows that German and English literature of the sixteenth and seventeenth centuries owes much to the emblematic attitude of mind and emblematic principles of composition. Sharrock's study focuses on the emblem as a literary device in *The Pilgrim's Progress*, while Rosemary Freeman, whose work embraces the English emblematic tradition, includes a discussion of the *Divine Emblems* as well as a study of the emblematic device in various works of Bunyan. An older work which also contains helpful insights on the earliest emblem writer is Henry Green, *Andrea Alciati and His Book of Emblems* (London, 1872). Mario Praz, *Studies in Seventeenth Century Imagery*, II (London, 1947) contains an excellent bibliography of emblem books.

2. Green, *Andrea Alciati*, pp. 113, 116, 247.

3. Van der Noot's *A Theatre for Worldlings*, has been described on occasion as the first emblem book printed in English. In 1569, Henry Bynneman brought out an English version of the work, originally written in Flemish.

4. Quoted in Henry Estienne, *The Art of Making Devices*. Translated by Thomas Blount (London, 1646), p. 10.

5. See Freeman, *English Emblem Books*, pp. 9-36, 99-113.

6. The ninth edition of 1724 contained woodcuts for the first time.

7. Frye, *Anatomy of Criticism*, p. 74.

8. D.W. Robertson Jr., *A Preface to Chaucer* (Princeton, 1960), p. 63.

9. Ibid.

10. Mario Praz, *Studies in Seventeenth Century Imagery*, I, (London, 1939), pp. 156-7.

11. Robertson, *A Preface to Chaucer*, p. 63.

12. Erwin Panofsky, *Studies in Iconology* (New York, 1967), is exceptionally helpful in showing how configuration of known things or objects stimulates insight into and understanding of an underlying order (see especially pp. 3-16). See also Bernard F. Huppé, *Doctrine and Poetry* (New York, 1959).

13. Daly, *Literature in Light of the Emblem*, p. 32.

14. *The Entire Works of John Bunyan*, Stebbing, Vol. 3, p. 221.

15. Emile Mâle, *Religious Art* (New York, 1968), p. 64.

16. *The Fathers of the Church*, II, Saint Augustine IV, 'Christian Instruction', trans. John J. Gavigan OSA (New York, 1947), pp.. 82-3.

17. Sharrock, 'Bunyan and the English Emblem Writers', p. 112.

18. 'Emblem and Interpretation in *The Pilgrim's Progress*', ELH, *33* (1966), p. 301.

19. Sharrock, 'Bunyan and the English Emblem Writers', p. 116.

20. *The Pilgrim's Progress*, ed. James Blanton Wharey, rev. Roger Sharrock (Oxford, 1960), p. 199.

21. Bunyan, *The Pilgrim's Progress*, pp. 199-200.

22. Daly, *Literature in Light of the Emblem*, p. 173.

23. Sharrock, 'Bunyan and the English Emblem Writers', p. 116.

24. 'Mercy With her Mirror', *Philological Quarterly*, XLII (1963), pp. 121-6.

25. 'The Cult of the Poet in Renaissance Emblem Literature', PMLA, LIX (September 1944), pp. 681-3.

26. See Praz, *Seventeenth Century Imagery*, pp. 103-4, 112-13, and 117-19 for discussion of various emblematists' use of specialised association of rose and lily.

27. Freeman, *English Emblem Books*, p. 214.

28. See Panofsky, *Studies in Iconology*, pp. 82-3.

29. Henry Green, ed. *Whitney's 'Choice of Emblemes'* (London, 1866).

30. Quotations are from *A Book for Boys and Girls*, a facsimile of the unique first edition, published in 1686 (London, 1890).

31. J. Paul Hunter, *The Reluctant Pilgrim*, p. 22.

32. James Blanton Wharey, ed. *The Pilgrim's Progress* (Oxford, 1960), p. 4.

7 THE SERMON-TREATISE

In his work *On Christian Doctrine*, Augustine gives directions to the 'expositor and teacher of the Divine Scripture'; he says:

> If those who hear are to be taught, exposition must be composed, if it is needed, that they may become acquainted with the subject at hand. In order that those things which are doubtful may be made certain, they must be reasoned out with the use of evidence. But if those who hear are to be moved rather than taught, so that they may not be sluggish in putting what they know into practice and so that they may fully accept those things which they acknowledge to be true, there is need for greater powers of speaking. Here entreaties and reproofs, exhortations and rebukes, and whatever devices are necessary to move minds must be used.[1]

Augustine thus shows the need to expound, to teach, to reason, and by 'whatever devices are necessary' to move minds so that lives practise what 'Divine Scripture' teaches. To accomplish desired ends in the exposition of Scripture, Augustine recognises that a sense of ordered structure is essential and his approach to the Scriptures includes principles that determined the character of education during the thousand years we rather unjustly call 'the Middle Ages', an approach still an important part of Christian humanism in the Renaissance.[2]

It is, of course, futile to argue that John Bunyan exercises the same profound influence on education as did Augustine, but that he has a deep desire to expound, to teach, to reason, and to move to action is evident from the way he shapes and moulds his sermon-treatises into a coherent pattern.

In examining the qualities which characterise the structure of his sermons, one might seek to determine to what extent Bunyan appropriates the fourfold method which preachers and Biblical scholars frequently use in the medieval era. Students of Scripture interpret it on four levels: the literal, allegorical, tropological, and anagogical. The literal restates the passage being considered; the allegorical shows the way in which the Biblical text points to general truths pertaining to humanity as a whole; the tropological explains the moral lessons to be gleaned from the text; and the anagogical suggests the ultimate meaning and significance of the Biblical passage.[3]

A fourfold interpretation of Psalm 114[4] illustrates the procedure:

When Israel went forth out of Egypt,
The house of Jacob from a people
of strange language;
Judah became his sanctuary
Israel his dominion.
The sea saw it and fled;
The Jordan was driven back.
The mountains skipped like rams,
The little hills like lambs.
What aileth thee, O thou sea, that thou fleest?
Thou Jordan, that thou turnest back?
Ye mountains, that ye skip like rams;
Ye little hills, like lambs?
Tremble, thou earth, at the pres-
ence of the Lord,
At the presence of the God of Jacob,
Who turned the rock into a pool
of water.
The flint into a fountain of waters.[5]

Taking this psalm as the Biblical text for his sermon, a preacher might begin by a literal explanation of the song in its historical context, the exodus of the Hebrew people from the strange land of Egypt to the sanctuary they found in Israel. He could then move to the allegorical level by suggesting that the exodus includes any individual of any land that leaves estrangement and seeks refuge. The tropological or moral lesson includes God's demands for reverence from man and nations, and the anagogical expounds the spiritual truth that God provides in miraculous ways for those who reverence and obey him.

If he is aware of the fourfold interpretation, Bunyan shows no strict adherence to the approach, but a few sermons bear the imprint of this method. *The Holy City*, or *The New Jerusalem*, for example, based on a lengthy text from the Book of the Revelation, Chapter XXI; 10-28; XXII; 1-4, begins with a discussion under six headings of the literal setting of the verses which entail the vision which John, the apostle, saw, proceeds from a vision of one particular apostle to a city which includes the 'whole family in heaven and earth', expands upon the moral lesson that any member of the New Jerusalem must bow to God's authority, and anagogically explains that the New Jerusalem or the holy city is prepared by God's 'strange judgements' and 'works of wonder'. Finally the way for man to become an inhabitant of that city is to regard and reverence these judgements and wonders.

The majority of Bunyan's sermons are similar to the structure stipulated in the preaching manual by the Elizabethan preacher, William Perkins, in his *Arte of Prophecying*, a title which associates the role of the preacher with that of the prophet who by his 'arte' properly presents and interprets Scripture. Perkins' structural model entails: opening the text, stating the doctrine, giving reasons as proofs, and finally offering uses and applications. A summary of his method embraces four major points:

1.   To reade the Text distinctly out of the Canonicall Scriptures.
2.   To give the sense and understanding of it being read, by the Scripture it selfe.
3.   To collect a few and profitable points of doctrine out of the naturall sense.
4.   To apply (if we have the gift) the doctrines rightly collected, to the life and manner of men, in a simple and plaine speech.[6]

Perkin's model is similar to those found in practically all of the subsequent manuals for Puritan preachers of the seventeenth century.[7] The various manuals may appear to suggest stereotyped sermons, but as Barbara Lewalski notes the appeal is to Biblical texture and style as 'the model for, or at least a determinant of, the preacher's appropriate art. This appeal does not lead to artlessness, or to the abnegation of art in the presentation of sacred subject matter . . . '[8]

In his earliest and one of his most sulphureous sermons, *Sighs from Hell* (1658), Bunyan closely follows the model suggested by Perkins. He chooses the parable of the rich man and Lazarus recorded in Luke 14: 19-31 as his text. Not completely keeping his promise that he 'will not be tedious' and that he will 'pass briefly through the several verses', he proceeds from verse to verse as he works out 'reasons' and 'proofs' and follows with 'uses' and 'applications', stating again that 'there might many things be spoken by way of use and application, but I shall be very brief' (I, p. 158). The one pervading theme is the horror of lostness. Through words denoting mental anguish like 'a never dying worm; and 'the unquenchable fire', Bunyan underscores the finality of lostness. Juxtaposed with lostness is judgement, and even in his lengthy digressions and meanderings he keeps before the reader the 'doctrine' of judgement. In the section of the parable, for example, 'Send Lazarus that he may dip the tip of his finger in water and cool my tongue', he digresses on that 'unruly member' of the human body, the tongue, with rhetorical questions and conversational persuasion; he concludes with a question from the book of James, 'For, I say unto you every idle word that men shall speak, they shall give account thereof in the day of judgement', thus keeping in the forefront of the sermon the crucial fact that the one crying out for Lazarus to 'dip the tip of his finger in water' and cool his parched tongue has already faced judgement. Chains of arguments and proofs link together lostness, death, and judgement. Intertwined with God's judgement is his grace; particularly in the 'application' is there the urgent plea for man to consider now his need for grace in light of the counsel and forewarning which the text affords.

It is worth observing that throughout the structured sermons, Bunyan demonstrates a highly effective manner of persuading his listeners to imagine themselves placed in a particular, concrete situation. Consider the graphic picture of the intolerable torments of the damned:

> ... thou shalt have none but a company of damned souls, with an innumerable company of devils to keep company with thee; while thou art in this world the very thought of the devils appearing to thee makes thy flesh to tremble, and thine hair ready to stand upright on thy head. But, oh, what wilt thou do, when not only the supposition of the devils appearing, but the real society of all the devils of hell will be with thee howling and roaring, screeching and roaring in such a hideous manner, that thou wilt be even at thy wits' end, and be ready to run stark mad again for anguish and torment. (I, p. 141-2)

The dreadful torment is more than feeling and hearing:

thou shalt see thy friends, thy acquaintance, thy neighbours; nay it may be, thy father, thy mother, thy wife, thy husband, thy children . . . when you shall see Abraham (your father), Isaac, and Jacob . . . and all the prophets in the Kingdom of heaven, and you yourselves thrust out . . . then for thy sins and disobedience shalt be shut, nay thrust out. (I, p. 141)

The scene becomes more and more expansive as paragraph follows paragraph: 'Unspeakable' torments of 'a never dying worm', of an 'oven fire', the 'fiery-furnace', 'the bottomless pit', the 'stream of fire'. From whatever point contemplated the anguish of the tormented is the gloomiest of all visions for human thought: the tortures of memory, the agonies of aloneness, the sorrows of desolation.

But Bunyan has yet another angle to examine: the desperate lot of the tormented must be seen in relation to eternity. By stacking spatial images on top of each other, Bunyan shows the enormity and finality of the ungodly's lost condition: 'when thou hast been in hell so many thousand years as there are stars in the firmament, or drops in the sea, or sands on the sea-shore, yet thou hast to *lie* there forever. Oh, this one word, Ever, how it will torment thy soul' (I, p. 142). The concrete situation, vividly built into the structure, takes on a panoramic sweep as Bunyan stretches it from infinity to infinity, and then with a final brush he admonishes the hearer to accept God's mercy. The emotional tensions of man in a specific situation with anguish intensifying and enlarging and with the scene moving from the perspective of eternity where there is no possible hope to temporal time where there is abundant mercy all make for an enormous, sweeping pictorial passage.

Perhaps an even more clearly marked example of the same structure of *Sighs from Hell* is that of *The Doctrine of Law and Grace Unfolded*. Not particularly heeding the advice of another author of a preaching manual, Joseph Glanvill, that 'divisions be not numerous, minute and nice' and that one of the worst offences in preaching is that 'of dividing Texts into indivisibles; and mincing them into single words',[9] John Bunyan selects the text, 'But ye are not under the law, but under grace.' He opens with a brief statement of the text in context of the three preceding chapters of the book of Romans. He then proceeds to the two doctrines: 'Doctrine 1. That there are some in gospel times that are under the covenant of works. Doctrine 2. That there is never a believer under the law, as it is the covenant of works, but under grace, through Christ . . .' (I, p. 185). Then come almost 60 pages of subdivisions with proofs, objections, questions, answers. The labels of the first doctrine include 'What the Covenant of Works is and When Given', 'Who They are That are under the Covenant of Works, What Men may obtain to that are under The Covenant of Works'. Then, he turns to his second doctrine, 'The New Covenant made with Christ', and subdivides: 'The Conditions of the New Covenant', 'The Suretyship of Christ', 'Christ the Messenger of the New Covenant', 'Christ the Sacrifice of the New Covenant', 'Christ the High Priest of the New Covenant', 'Christ the Forerunner of the Saints', and reaches finally his climactic section, 'Christ Completely Fulfilled the Conditions of the New Covenant'. He turns next to opposers of the Covenant of Grace, labelling each step, and then proceeds to 'A Use of Examination About the Old Covenant' and 'The Use of the New Covenant', saving ultimately a little space for application of his rather laboriously drawn explication (I, pp. 186-259).

Closely associated with the textual opening and 'doctrine-uses-application' model is another which Bunyan frequently uses. First, there is an introduction in which he places the biblical passage in its context. Thus in *The Resurrection of the Dead*, he states the text: 'But this I confess unto thee, that after the way which they call heresy, so worship I the God of my fathers, believing all things which are written in the law and the prophets. And have hope towards God, which they themselves, also allow, that there shall be a resurrection of the dead, both of the just and unjust' (Acts XXIV, 14, 15). He then briefly gives the focus of his discourse, and losing no time, places the passage in its historical context: 'Paul being, upon his arraignment, accused of many things, by some that were violent for his blood; and being licensed to speak for himself by the then heathen magistrate, he doth in few words tell them . . . he was utterly faultless, only this he confessed, that after that way which they call heresy, so he worshipped the God of his fathers . . .' (I, p. 340).

There follow preliminary remarks concerning the various meanings of the resurrection of the dead, and then he shows the major two-fold structure of his framework. First he will prove the resurrection of the just and then he will turn to the resurrection of the wicked, with both aspects of the structure containing specifically labelled subpoints.

In this way the listener and the reader can see at a glance the general direction the sermon will take and the topics to be covered. As Henri Talon aptly states, 'here, too, side by side, with his own born orator's instinct, Bunyan was following in the tradition of all sacred oratory, whether popular or learned, whether addressed to simple people or to the lettered'.[10] And we need only turn to John Donne's sermons to see how acutely aware one of the most lettered preachers of the age was of structure. In his first extant sermon preached on 30 April 1615, at Greenwich, on the biblical passage from Isaiah 52:3, 'Ye have sold your selves for nought, and ye shall be redeemed without money', Donne's structure consists of an introduction, a division, and the principal parts referred to in the division. The introduction delineates three main interpretations by commentators upon the text. After careful discussion of the three interpretations, Donne proceeds to an analysis of each word of the text, giving detailed study to the words, 'nought', 'without money', and 'redeemed'.

There follows a 'Divisio', a statement of the two main parts into which the sermon is to be divided: '*Exprobrationem*, and *Consolationem*: First, an exprobration, or increpation from God to us, and then a consolation, or consolidation of the same God upon us.' The first principal part is then divided into two subpoints: '... in the exprobration, God reproaches to us, first, our Prodigality, that we would sell a reversion, our possibility, our expectance of an inheritance in heaven; And then, our cheapness, that we would sell that, for nothing.' The first subpoint, discussing prodigality, is in turn divided into three parts each of which describes the adversities or misfortunes befalling the prodigal (I, p. 154).[11] From sermon to sermon, the number of the divisions varies, as does the number of subpoints, but the sermon preached at Greenwich shows John Donne's awareness of sermon structure.

Few, if any, preachers of the seventeenth century could equal the eloquence and artistry of John Donne, yet for him, the eloquence of the Scripture is the model for an eloquent, artistic sermon. He states in one of his sermons:

> Religious preaching is a grave exercise, but not a sordid, not a barbarous, not a negligent. There are not so eloquent books in the world as the Scriptures ... Whatsoever hath justly delighted any man in any man's writings, is exceeded in the Scriptures. The style of the Scriptures is a diligent ... style; and a great part thereof in a musical, in a metrical, in a measured composition,

in verse . . . So the Holy Ghost hath spoken in those Instruments, whom he chose for the penning of the Scriptures, and so
he would in those whom he sends for the preaching thereof . . .
Then are we . . . music to the soul, in the manner of our preaching, when in delivering points of Divinity we content ourselves
with that language, and that phrase of speech, which the Holy
Ghost hath expressed himself in, in the Scriptures.[12]

Bunyan would unquestionably agree that the Bible should provide the primary model for the sermon and that no other work can
equal its eloquence, beauty, and artistry. But Bunyan would be
among those who find 'the scripture style characterized not by
witty and eloquent figures but by much simpler and more direct
rhetorical strategies conveying its powerful message to audiences
of all kinds and capacities'.[13]

The style or rhetoric of a well-constructed sermon was, in fact,
the subject of controversy. John Downame, for example, speaks
for others in asserting that 'the holie Ghost in penning the Scripture hath used great simplicitie and wonderful plainnesse'.[14]
George Herbert, Public Orator at Cambridge, poet, and minister
of the village church of Bemerton, argues in his *Priest to the Temple*
that the preacher be 'not witty, or learned, or eloquent, but Holy'
and that the model for his rhetoric be the Scriptures. The preacher
should also choose 'moving and ravishing texts, whereof the Scriptures are full' and should also follow the example of Scriptures in
choosing illustrations drawn from familiar objects like 'a plough,
a hatchet, a bushell, leaven, boyes piping and dancing'.[15] Furthermore, Herbert desires a twofold division of a text in a strongly constructed sermon to include a statement of the text's central
meaning and comments on the text as a whole, and he castigates
the custom of 'crumbling a text into small parts . . .'[16] John Wilkins
speaks against 'Rhetorical flourishes' and takes the position that
the 'greatest learning is to be seen in the greatest plainness'.[17]
Robert South exhorts preachers to speak with 'unaffected plainness and simplicity' and contends that Biblical truth should be
presented 'in the plainnest and most intelligible language'.[18]

Bunyan subdivides and probably 'crumbles the text' in many
sermons, and certainly he writes or speaks all of them in a plain
style, but the structure varies. In addition to models already cited,
he also works out an entire sermon around a central figure or a
parable.

An example of organising around one central figure is his sermon
on the scriptural passage, 'So run that ye may obtain' (I Cor. ix, 24).
Entitled *The Heavenly Footman*, the work shows the route to
heaven and a race to be run — and won. In an early section.
Bunyan writes:

> These words, they are taken from men's running for a wager; a
> very apt similitude to set before the eyes of the saints of the Lord.
> Know ye not that they which run in a race run all, but one
> receiveth the prize? So run, that ye may obtain? That is, do not
> only run, but be sure you win as well as run . . . The prize is
> heaven, and if you will have it, you must run for it. (IV, p.
> 180)

Keeping the central figure clearly before the reader, he shows, as
he 'opens' the word, run, that it is a 'fleeing' for one's life, a 'pressing' through 'all that may stand between heaven and their souls',
and a 'continuing' to 'run', to 'run through all difficulties', and 'to
continue to the end of the race' (IV, p. 180). Following the 'opening'
of the central figure, he then gives seven reasons for 'clearing this
doctrine' of the runner: because every one who runs does not
obtain ('there are some professors do not go on so fast in the way of
God as a snail doth go on the wall', IV, p. 180); because if they do
not obtain, then they will lose their running also (if the man who
runs does not win the prize, 'he doth lose his labor, spend his pains
and time, and that to no purpose', IV, p. 180); because the way is
long, ('there is many a dirty step, many a high hill', IV, p. 181);
because the time is uncertain (' . . . the bell may toll for thee before
seven days more be ended', IV, p. 181); because the devil, sin, hell,
and the law run after them (' . . . the devil is nimble, he can run
apace . . . the law can shoot a great way . . . hell can stretch itself
farther than you are aware of', IV, p. 181); because heaven's gates
may be shut shortly (' . . . if they be shut . . . they are so heavy that all
the men in the world, nor all the angels in heaven, are not able to
open them', IV, p. 118); and because if the runner loses, he loses all
('thou losest soul, God, Christ, heaven, ease, peace . . .', IV, p.
182).

At the end of each of the seven reasons for 'clearing the doctrine', there is a repetition of the word, 'run', which underscores in
a refrain-like manner the central figure. Then follow nine directions
on 'how to run so as to obtain', then come nine 'motives' for running

the race followed by nine 'uses' or examinations to determine whether or not the runners are earnestly running the race in order to obtain the prize. This earnestness embraces anything that hinders, for the runner must run 'continually', and 'strip off everything that would hinder in his race...' (IV, p. 189). The book closes with a 'provocation' to 'run with the foremost' and an 'expostulation' to begin the race, to 'run apace, and hold out to the end, and the Lord give ... a prosperous journey' (IV, p. 192).

In another sermon Bunyan works out an allegory around the parable of the barren fig tree. He structures his work, *The Barren Fig Tree*, on the account in Luke XIII: 6-9:

> A certain man had a fig-tree planted in his vineyard; and he came and sought fruit thereon, and found none. Then said he unto the dresser of his vineyard, Behold, these three years I come seeking fruit on this fig-tree, and find none: cut it down; why cumbereth it on the ground? And, he answering said unto him, Lord, let it alone this year also, till I dig about it, and dung it; and if it bear fruit, well; and if not, then after that thou shalt cut it down.

'The metaphors', says Bunyan, 'in this parable are, 1. A certain man; 2. A vineyard; 3. A fig-tree, barren or fruitless; 4. A dresser; 5. Three years; 6. Digging and dunging... The doctrine, or mystery couched under these words, is to show us what is like to become of a fruitless or formal professor' (II, p. 248). Before developing the sermon, he first identifies the figures: a certain man is God, the vineyard is the church, the fig-tree is the fruitless professor, the dresser is Jesus, the three years define the time limit of God's patience, the digging and dunging are attempts to make the barren tree fruitful, and the calling to the dresser to cut down the tree shows 'outcries of justice' against barren professors. Of central importance in the teaching of the New Testament is the metaphor of the Christian as bearer of appropriate fruit. Consider the text, Matthew 7: 16-17, 'Ye shall know them by their fruits. Do men gather grapes of thorns or figs of thistles? / Even so every good tree bringeth forth fruit; but a corrupt tree bringeth forth evil fruit.' Closely related to this text is the parable that Bunyan chooses as the organising metaphor for his sermon-treatise, and through a variety of 'signs', he vividly shows the meaning and significance of the figures in the parable:

Barren fig-tree, hearken; the continual non-bearing of fruit is a dreadful sign ... Barren fig-tree, fruitless professor, hast thou heard all these things? Hast thou considered that this fig-tree is not acknowledged of God to be his, but is denied of his planting ... Barren fig-tree, dost thou hear? God expected fruit, God calls for fruit; yea, God will shortly come seeking fruit on this barren fig-tree ... there is a fruit among professors that withers, and so never comes to ripe ... There is a hasty fruit ... that runs up suddenly, violently with great stalks and big show, and yet at last proves empty of kernel ... There is a fruit that is vile and ill-tasted ... There is a fruit that is wild ... there is also untimely fruit ... God expecteth fruit that shall answer that faith which thou makest profession of ... God expecteth fruits according to the seasons of Grace thou art under ... Barren fig-tree, God expects it, and will find it too, if ever he bless thee ... Barren soul, how many showers of grace, how many dews from heaven, how many times have the silver streams of the city of God run gliding by thy roots, to cause thee to bring forth fruit ... fruits that become thy profession of the Gospel, the God of Heaven expecteth. (II, p. 250-4)

To punctuate lengthy expositions, Bunyan frequently organises large parts of his sermons around the 'objection–answer' or 'question–answer' structure. A brief section from *Some Gospel Truths Opened* illustrates the objection — answer device:

Quest. But did this Man rise again from the dead, that very man, with that very body wherewith he was crucified? for you do seem, as I conceive, to hold forth so much by these your expressions.
Ans.   Why do you doubt of it?
Quest.   Do you believe it?
Ans.   Yes, by the grace of the Lord Jesus Christ, for he hath enabled me so to do.
Quest.   And can you prove it by the Scripture?
Ans.   Yes.
Quest.   How?
Ans.   First, from that scripture in Luke XXIV, 37-41 ... Many other scriptures could I give for the proof ...
Quest.   Why did he rise again from the dead with that very body?

Ans. Because it was not possible he should be holden of death. (I, p. 83)

Pointed exchanges like these, suggestive of lively, zealous, intense conversation, lend not only a sense of firm purpose but revive the sense of immediacy frequently obscured by long arguments and indicate the potential presence of two clashing individuals behind the questions and answers. All the qualities of dialogue which Bunyan used effectively and dramatically in his major works are here in embryo: the terse manageableness, the suggested immediacy, and the externalisation of inner conflicts.

Occasionally, Bunyan organises sermons around a well-known concept. Central to his sermon entitled *Christian Behaviour* is the concept of hierarchy, or the pervasive idea of order and degree. This is by no means a new thought in Bunyan, for the idea of a hierarchical cosmos is older than the Christian religion, but Christianity gave it, with various modifications, additional support. According to the hierarchical view, everything and everyone except God has a superior. Beneath God the hierarchy is as follows: angelic creatures, men, animals, plants, inorganic matter, and finally chaos. Within a given rank there are subhierarchies: just as God is the highest spiritual being, so the sun is the chief planet, the king is the chief human being, the lion is king of the beasts, gold is the best metal. Christian thinkers see the idea of order, for example, in Romans 13:1, 'Let every soul be subject to the higher power', and in 13:7, 'Render therefore to all their dues: tribute to whom tribute is due; custom to whom custom, fear to whom fear; honour to whom honour.'

Writers of both the sixteenth and seventeenth centuries show a preoccupation with the idea of order: sermons on the topic were officially prepared and designated to be read in the churches, and one of the greatest dramatists of the era, or of all time, William Shakespeare, shows an understanding of the prevailing concept. It is true, of course, that speeches in Shakespeare like those of the Gardener (III, iv, 29-66) and Carlisle (IV, i, 115-38) in *Richard II* or Ulysses in *Troilus and Cressida* (I, iii, 78-135) or Menenius in *Coriolanus* (I, i, 97-156) exist in a dramatic context. The characters deliver their speeches on order not because Shakespeare especially wishes to preach the doctrine but because the concept suits a particular speaker's purpose at a specific dramatic moment. It is not inaccurate, however, to assume that the concept of order is frequently on Shakespeare's mind. After all, the genre in which he writes focuses on conflict and the disruption of order.

In one of his more beautiful sermons, Bunyan strongly affirms his belief in a concept of order. In 'The Epistle to the Reader', which immediately precedes his sermon, *Christian Behaviour*, Bunyan states as one of his reasons for writing the book the following:

> . . . it is amiable and pleasant to God when Christians keep their rank, religion, and station, doing all as becometh their quality and calling. When Christians stand everyone in their places, and do the work of their relations, then they are like the flowers in the garden, that stand and grow where the gardener hath planted them, and then they shall both honour in which they are planted, and the gardener that hath so disposed of them. (II, p. 164)

He also promises that he will 'fall upon those things' that he judges 'most necessary for the people of God' (II, p. 165) or for those who live by the principle of Faith, which Bunyan calls '. . . so great an artist in arguing and reasoning with the soul' (II, p. 166). Then he begins to write of the various responsibilities of those who 'stand and grow where the gardener hath planted them.' Addressing first the duties of the 'master of the family', Bunyan sees those responsibilities as analogous to those of a pastor. Just as a pastor must be sound and uncorrupt in doctrine, should be apt to teach, to reprove and to exhort, and must himself be exemplary in faith and holiness, and of the church, so also should the 'master of the family'.

From the general duties, 'the master of the family' is to love his wife as his own flesh and as a joint heir of 'the grace of life'. He is to carry himself 'to and before her, as doth Christ to and before his church . . .' (II, p. 171). 'One of the chief ends in instituting marriage,' says Bunyan, is 'that Christ and his church, under a figure, might be wherever there is a couple that believe through grace' (II, p. 172). The 'station' of wives is, though in subjection to the husband, not to be 'their husbands' slaves' but 'yoke-fellows', and since 'the believing woman is a figure of the church, she ought, as the church, to nourish and instruct her children and servants as the church . . . ' (II, p. 174-6).

If couples bear children then they must consider the full responsibility of that calling. They are to instruct them and to correct them (and 'see if fair words will win them from evil', for this is 'God's way with his children', II, p. 173), and they must take heed that 'the misdeeds for which thou correctest thy children be not learned them by thee' (II, p. 173).

The master's duties extend also to servants, and one of the chief responsibilities is to treat them as human beings and not turn them into slaves, 'by overcharging them in thy work, through thy greediness'. To behave so that the servant may work not only for the good of the master but for the good of the servant in both body and soul is one of Bunyan's primary injunctions.

Children have a 'station' too, and they have a duty to parents to obey them and to honour them. Bunyan holds that there are three things for which, as long as children live, they are debtors to their parents:

1. For thy being in this world. They are they from whom immediately under God, thou didst receive it [life].
2. For their care to preserve thee when thou wast helpless, and couldst neither care for nor regard thyself.
3. For the pains they have taken with thee to bring thee up (II, p. 176).

To Bunyan, it 'is worse than heathenish' that children neglect parents or 'have slighting and scornful thoughts of them' (II, p. 176). To dishonour parents is to disrupt order and to act as though one has 'the heart of a dog or a beast, that will bite those that begot them, and her that brought them forth' (II, p. 176).

'Servants', also, says Bunyan, '. . . have a work to do for God, in their place and station among men' (II, p. 177). He thinks of the general duties as threefold:

1. Thou art to look upon thyself as thou art, that is, a servant, not a child, nor a wife; thou art inferior to these; wherefore count thyself under them and be content with that station . . .
2. Consider, that thou being a servant, what is under thy hand is not thy own, but thy master's. Now, because it is not thy own thou oughtest to dispose of it; but because it is thy master's thou oughtest to be faithful . . .
3. Touching thy work and employment, thou art to do it as unto the Lord, and not for men; and indeed then servants

do their business as becomes them, when they do all in obedience to the Lord, as knowing that the place in which they now are,
it is the place where Christ hath put them . . . (II, p. 176).

Combining varieties of 'stations', Bunyan next speaks of
neighbours. Qualities which characterise this orderly place
include: good and sound conversation, courtesy and charity,
humility and meekness, graciousness, and wisdom. To practise
these qualities is one way of 'asserting the things of God' to others
and, at the same time, of edifying members of the neighbourhood.

Although John Bunyan organises the sermon, *Christian Behaviour*,
around the concept of hierarchy, he does not deprecate or demean
the significance or the place of any human being. Each has a place
in the nurture and nourishment of the other. A clear and beautiful
statement towards the close of the treatise substantiates the importance of all:

Christians are like the several flowers in a garden, that have
upon each of them the dew of heaven, which being shaken with
the wind, they let fall their dew at each other's roots, whereby
they are jointly nourished, and become nourishers of one
another . . . (II, p. 183)

A less frequent mode of structure is the building of an entire sermon
around several chapters from Scripture. *An Exposition of the First
Ten Chapters of Genesis* is a chief example of this structure, and one
which permits Bunyan to discuss many subjects which seem to
fascinate him throughout his ministry. A topic central to
numerous sermons is the work and person of God and the distinctiveness, yet unity, of the members of the Trinity; it is with this
central topic that Bunyan begins. Within the sermon there is an
extended analogy between God's work in the six days of creation
and various characteristic qualities of man's spiritual life. The first
days, when 'the Spirit of God moved upon the face of the earth' is
analogous to the beginning of spiritual regeneration. Bunyan
says:

A blessed emblem of the Word of God is the matter of regeneration: for as the first chaos remained without form, and void,
until the Spirit of God moved to work upon it, and by working,
to put this world into frame and order; so man as he comes into

the world, abides a confused lump, an unclean thing; a creature without New Testament order, until by the Spirit of the Lord he is transformed into the image of Jesus Christ. (III, p. 373)

On that first day of creation God moves upon the waters and makes light, so the first day of man's spiritual regeneration is the illumination he has of himself and of God through the light of the Word. 'His first word in order to our conversion is,' says Bunyan, ' "Let there be light", light, to see their state by nature; light to see the fruits and effects of sin; light to see the truth and worth of the merits of Jesus Christ; light to see the truth and faithfulness of God . . .' (III, p. 373).

On the second day God makes the firmament and separates the waters under the firmament from those above it; those waters under the firmament 'figure out the world as ungodly', and those above it, represent 'the select and chosen of God'. Creation on the second day signifies the two 'great peoples' of the world, the godly and the ungodly. God's order of the third day that the waters be gathered in one place to permit the dry land to appear signifies the 'thrifty church of God', says Bunyan, and the Church is in a flourishing state 'when the world is farthest from her, and when the roaring of their waves are far away' (III, p. 375).

The creations of the fourth day include the lights in the firmament of heaven, or the sun, moon, and stars. The sun parallels the Christ, who is the 'true light of the world' and of the church; the moon, although it changes, increases and diminishes, signifies the regenerate Christians, the Church, in 'her uncertain conditions in this world', and the stars show how innumerable are the saints, 'those spiritual stars shall be' and how 'they shall differ each from other in glory' (III, p. 375). The creation of moving and living creatures on the fifth day primarily denotes the varieties of persecutors, small and great, capable of preying on the dedicated Christian. Finally, the creation of the sixth day, the creation of man, 'this wonderful piece of the workmanship of God' (III, p. 376) is made in the likeness of God; yet man is only a shadow of a more excellent image, Christ, who alone is the express image of God. Man, though glorious, is a creature, subject to all the limitations of finiteness, but in the 'express image of God', he finds one who not only brings him into his spiritual state but also gives hope for immortality at the end of life. '. . . As He [Christ] is called,' says Bunyan, ' "an image", he is also called, "the first born of every creature" .. his being a creature, respecting his manhood, and his birth, his rising again from the dead . . . he is called "the first-born from the dead" ' (III, p. 377). Each day of creation is thus viewed as analogous to various aspects of man's spiritual life.

If he had closed his sermon with the analogy in which the stages of the beginning and development of the spiritual life is made clearer through its comparison to the six days of creation, Bunyan would have written one of his most strongly unified treatises. What he does, however, is to work out additional analogies from subsequent views and chapters. The water of the flood, for example, is analogous to three things: enemies of the church, water-baptism under the New Testament, and 'the last and general overthrow of the world' (III, p. 416). But he also returns to his original preoccupation with a comparison of the creation to the spiritual state of man. When he discusses God's injunction to Noah and his sons to 'be fruitful and multiply, and replenish the earth' (Genesis IX: 1), Bunyan thinks of the command as analogous to those

> who are brought into the Kingdom of Christ . . . not to be idle, but to be fruitful, and to labour to fill the world with a spiritual seed to God: for as Noah, so are we made heirs of this blessed Kingdom; and shall also, as that good man, leave, when we sleep in Jesus, this spiritual seed to possess the Kingdom after us. (III, p. 436)

Thus, Bunyan in a rather complex sentence constructs an analogy that sees one injunction as analogous to the entrance into the Christian life, the work of the Christian in his mortal life, the fact of death which closes life, and the truth of immortality which awaits spiritual man.

If he could build sermons around numerous chapters, so also could he construct them around one word. Selecting the text, 'And if anyone sin, we have an advocate with the Father, Jesus Christ the righteous' (I John 2:1), Bunyan makes use of what he calls 'the similitude or office of an advocate' and organises the treatise around the one word, advocate. To show readers the 'many and singular advantages' they have 'by this their advocate', he says himself that he will give an account of 'where the advocate pleads, how he pleads, what he pleads, when he pleads, with whom he pleads, for whom he pleads . . .' (IV, p. 313). He further delineates how individuals may know how 'to entertain this advocate to plead their cause and he promises that this advocate 'never lost a cause, nor a soul, for whom he undertook to be an advocate...' and his powerful capacity to plead a case puts the enemy to 'shame and silence before...God and all the holy angels' (IV, p. 313). Christ, as advocate, is a distinctive office, for Bunyan says at the conclusion of his closely-knit arguments: 'He died for all his elect, he prayeth for his elect as a priest; but as an advocate he pleadeth only for the children, the CALLED only' (IV, p. 358). As Richard L. Greaves states: 'This calling was the result of election — of being ordained to eternal life; it was the "Fruit of electing Love".'[19]

For approximately 50 years Bunyan's active mind presented the truths of the Christian faith, as he understood them in a variety of ways. The range of subjects is wide; many sermons focus primarily on man's need for salvation, but he also writes on the greatness of the soul, on the beauty of Christianity, and on the glory of the 'New Jerusalem', to mention only a few additional topics. Whatever his subject, there is at the centre of the sermon the scriptural text, and Bunyan's exposition never fails to include a demonstration of the relationship of the Word to human lives.

If Bunyan interprets texts from the Book of the Word and organises these texts into sermon-treatises, so also does he look to another of God's books, the book of creatures or the book of the world, for additional interpretative materials. He watches the toils of the coney and the spider; he observes the sun, moon and stars; he notices the flowers in an English garden and listens to songs of the birds; he beholds the habits of beasts of the field, and, in all of these as well as other features of the Book of the World sees something about God and about man.

Bunyan is not alone in his belief that the book of creatures, a metaphor that comes down from the Middle Ages,[20] contains spiritual significance. The idea of the existence of 'two books' that complement each other, the Bible and the book of creatures, is a topic of considerable discussion among other writers of the seventeenth century.

In one of his sermons, John Donne thinks of the book of the world or the book of creatures as a huge library in which man can read of God:

All other authors we distinguish by *tomes*, by *parts*, by *volumes*; but who knows the volumes of this Author; how many volumes of Spheares involve one another, how many tomes of God's

Creatures there are? Hast thou not room, hast thou not leasure, for great volumes, for the *bookes of heaven* (for the *Mathematiques*) nor for the books of *Courts* (The *Politiques*) take but the *Georgiques,* the consideration of the *Earth*, a farme . . . Goe lower; every *worme* in the grave . . . is an abridgment of all . . . a *worme*, a *weed*, thy *selfe*, thy *pulse*, thy *thoughts*, are all testimonies, that *All,* this *All,* and the parts thereof, are *Opus, a work made,* and *opus ejus, his work* made by *God.*[21]

What is especially significant in this statement is Donne's conviction that these various books point to an author, and the author is God. Even the worm in the grave is a testimony to God's authorship. Thus the book of creatures is a revelation of God:

Here God shows this inconsiderate man, his book of creatures, which he may run and reade; that is, he may go forward in his vocation, and yet see that every creature calls him to a consideration of God. Every Ant that he sees, askes him, Where had I this providence, and industry? Every flower that he sees, asks him, where had I this beauty, this fragrancy, this medicinall vertue in me? Every creature calls him to consider, what great things God hath done in little subjects.[22]

The creature, then, argues not only the existence of an author but also calls the serious observer to discover manifestations of God.

Similar to John Donne's view on the importance of the book of creatures, is John Calvin's position: 'This skillful ordering of the universe is for us a sort of mirror in which we can contemplate God, who is otherwise invisible . . . The most perfect way of seeking God . . . is . . . to contemplate him in his works whereby he renders himself near and familiar to us, and in some manner communicates himself.'[23] Calvin further contends, however, that the Fall has hampered man's capacity to glean the spiritual significance of the book of creatures; accordingly, he must first turn to Scripture, be illumined by the 'book of the Word' and then go to the 'book of the World' with a clearer understanding. But, this book of creatures has special importance for John Calvin as the following statements suggest:

Let us not be ashamed to take pious delight in the works of God open and manifest in this most beautiful theatre . . . There is no doubt that the Lord would have us uninterruptedly occupied in this holy meditation; that, while we contemplate in all creatures, as in mirrors, those immense riches of his wisdom, justice, goodness, and power, we should not merely run over them cursorily, . . . but we should ponder them at length.[24]

Both John Calvin and John Donne hold that the book of creatures reveals God and his divine attributes; both also believe that the book of the Word and the book of the World complement each other. 'The voyce of the Creature alone, is but a faint voyce, a low voyce; nor any voyce,' says Donne, 'till the voyce of the Word inanimate it; for then when the Word of God both taught us any mystery of our Religion, then the booke of creatures illustrates, and establishes, and cherishes that which we have received by faith, in hearing the Word . . .'[25]

Joining with Donne and Calvin in urging Christians to study the creatures as true manifestations of God's divine attributes is Richard Baxter. 'The World is Gods book, which he set man at first to read; and every Creature is a Letter, or Syllable, or Word, or Sentence,' says Baxter, 'more or less declaring the name and will of God. Then you may behold his wonderful Almightiness, his unsearchable Wisdom, his unmeasurable Goodness, mercy, and compassions, and his singular regard of the sons of men.'[26]

Seventeenth-century writers think of the book of creatures not only as a revelation of God and his attributes which Christians discover, but also as a rich source of moral lessons which serve as instruction in Christian behaviour. Joseph Hall states, for example, 'the creatures are halfe lost if wee only imploy them, not learne something of them: God is wronged if his creatures bee unregarded; our selves most of all, if wee read this great volume of the creatures, and take out no lesson for our instruction.'[27] In the same spirit of moral instruction, Robert Boyle suggests turning 'all kinds of Creatures in the world . . . not onely into Teachers of Ethicks, but oftentimes into Doctors of Divinity'.[28]

What these seventeenth-century writers suggest, then, is that the book of creatures contains objects which reveal something about God and also embody a source of moral and ethical lessons which Christians may apply to their lives. Both aspects have significance only if viewed through what Calvin calls the 'spectacles' of Scriptures. Barbara Lewalski, a contemporary scholar, makes a similar point: 'The guide and standard for both is scripture: the nature similes, metaphors, and parables in the Bible provide the key to the lesson or significances which the creatures present, and several biblical passages (for instance the Creation account in Genesis... Job 38, and Romans 8: 19-22) are persistently identified as . . . indices of appropriate topics for meditation.'[29]

In his sermon, *The Resurrection of the Dead*, John Bunyan shows in one succinct statement his agreement with seventeenth-century writers that the book of creatures serves a twofold purpose. He declares: '. . . the whole creation that is before thee are not only made to show the power of God in themselves, but also to teach thee, and to preach unto thee, both much of God and thyself...' (I, p. 363). In an equally cogent statement, he says: 'As the creation in general preacheth to every man something of God; so they do hold forth how man should behave, both to God and one to another...' (I, p. 363). Further pursuing his belief, Bunyan says:

> This book of the creatures, it is so excellent and so full, so easy, and so suiting the capacity of all, that there is not one man in the world but is ... convicted ... by it. This is the book, that he who knows no letters may read in; yea, and that he who neither saw New Testament nor Old, may know both much of God and himself by. It is this book, out of which generally both Job and his friends did so profoundly discourse of the judgments of God ... This is the book, out of which both Christ, the prophets, and apostles, do so frequently discourse by their similitudes, proverbs, and parables . . . (I, pp. 364-5)

If then, the book of creatures serves the suggested twofold purpose, what does the book reveal of God and how does it provide instruction for man? For Bunyan, it manifests the 'eternal power and Godhead' of the creator; it reveals 'God's righteousness and justice' (and he cites Romans I: 18-20 as evidence); it declares his 'wisdom', and 'in wisdom' God made all creatures; it shows God's 'loving-kindness' (he cites Psalms CVIII; CXI 2 for support), and it also reveals that God has 'by the book of the creatures... sealed the judgement of the world' (I, pp. 363-5). Thus Bunyan discovers in the book of creatures attributes of God, including his power, righteousness, wisdom, loving-kindness, and justice. To discover these attributes is important to Bunyan, but his greatest emphasis seems to be on the book-world figures not as manifestations or revelations of God's attributes but rather on lessons which they embody for moral instruction.

To Bunyan creatures show that they are content to follow a divine order; only man is restless and therefore unwilling to keep his place in God's plan. '... Even the very dragons, and all deeps, fire, hail, snow, and vapours,' says Bunyan, '... are all in subjection ... Thus ... by their obedience to God, they teach ...' (I, p. 363). To observe the obedience of creatures to 'all superiors' is a condemnation of man, 'for every kind of beasts, and of birds, and all serpents, and things in the sea is [*sic*] tamed, and hath been tamed, and brought into obedience by mankind. Man only remains untamed and unruly, and therefore by these are condemned' (I, p. 363).

Furthermore, man forgets that as a Christian he should be a fruitful Christian, but Bunyan reminds him to look to the 'fruitfulness of all creatures, in their kind' and be admonished to live a fruitful life. It is also in the habits of the creatures that man may observe knowledge and wisdom. 'The stork in the heaven, the swallow and the crane, by observing the time and season of their coming,' says Bunyan, 'do admonish thee to learn the time of grace, and of the mercy of God. The ox and the ass, by the knowledge they have of their master's crib, do admonish thee to know the bread and table of God; and both do and shall condemn thy ignorance of the good of heaven' (I, p. 364).

In the same didactic spirit, he urges man to observe the labour and toil of the ant, coney, and the spider; these creatures convict of sloth and idleness. Even the young ravens, depending upon God and loving their young, condemn man for lying, cheating, defrauding, and other similar sins.

What Bunyan declares is that the book of creatures may be read by any man. To neglect this book is to ignore manifestations of God as well as moral instruction in obedience, fruitfulness, wisdom, labour, and love that the book of creatures embodies. So seriously does Bunyan view the book of creatures that he contends that it is a constant reminder of man's need for God, and 'as inconsiderable and unlikely' as the creatures may appear to the observer, in the day of judgement they 'will be found the items and warning words of God to your souls' (I, p. 364).

Earlier, I referred to Bunyan's emblematic habit of mind in various writings as well as in his *Divine Emblems*; this same habit locates many objects in the Book of the World that enhance in his mind knowledge of moral and spiritual matters. He looks, for example, at the 'inferior courts of judicature', whose under-governors could be faulty, and contrasts it with the Throne of Heaven from which none can appeal; he views a bed and finds it to be an emblem of a grave; he observes a jail and discovers an emblem of the 'prison of hell'; he sees the herbs and flowers in the English garden and points to their counterfeits in the field and thinks of the latter to be those with 'wild faith' whom God never plants in his garden, the church.

In his sermon, *The Saint's Privilege and Profit*, he declares ' . . . a very fit emblem the rainbow is of the righteousness of Christ' (IV, p. 278). With apparent pleasure in the discovery of this emblem, Bunyan amplifies on its significance:

1. The rainbow is an effect of the sun that shines in the firmament; and the righteousness by which the throne of grace is encompassed is the work of the son of God.

2. The rainbow was a token that the wrath of God in sending the flood was appeased; this righteousness of Christ is that for the sake of which God forgiveth us all trespasses.

3. The rainbow was set in the cloud that the sinful man might look thereon and wax confident in common mercy; this righteousness is showed us in the word, that we may by it believe unto special mercy.

4. The bow is seen but now and then in the cloud; Christ's righteousness is but here and there revealed in the word.

5. The bow is seen commonly upon, or after rain; Christ's righteousness is apprehended by faith upon, or soon after the apprehension of wrath.

6. The bow is sometimes more, sometimes less; and so is this righteousness, even according to the degree of faith.

7. The bow is of that nature as to make whatever you shall look upon through it, to be of the same colour of itself . . . and the righteousness of Christ is that that makes sinners, when God looks upon them through it, to look beautiful, and acceptable in his sight . . . (IV, p. 278)

After he examines these seven facets of the rainbow as emblem, Bunyan finds difficulty in letting go of his discoveries, for he states, 'one word more of the rainbow' (IV, p. 278), then shows its place 'round the throne' which leads him to discuss the rainbow as an emblem of Christ as man's high priest before God's throne.

The Book of Creatures or the Book of Nature is, then, for Bunyan as for other seventeenth-century writers a manifestation or revelation of God which an observer discovers; it is equally a rich source of moral and spiritual lessons which one may apply to his own life. So important is this Book of Nature to the seventeenth-century mind that few would disagree with the state-ment of Sir Thomas Browne: 'Nature tels me I am the Image of God as well as Scripture; that he understands not thus much, hath not his introduction or first lesson, and is yet to begin the Alphabet of man.'[30]

If Bunyan shows interest in the Book of the World in his sermon-treatises, he also demonstrates clear appreciation of the symbolic mode practised by early patristic, medieval, and seventeenth-century exegetes. Without exploring here the con-troversy over the difference between allegory and typology, from the patristic writers to the Protestant Reformation,[31] I wish to submit that Bunyan shows his variant of the Protestant theory of typology, clearly formulated and widely accepted in the seventeenth century.

The theory emphasises that the types are the symbolic dimen-sion of the literal text, and that typology pertains to Old Testament persons, events, ceremonies and artifacts which foreshadow and which are fulfilled in the New Testament. In accepting typological symbolism, seventeenth-century thinkers also find a New Testa-ment warrant for the typological reading of various Old Testament passages. In Luke 11:30-31, Luke 17:26-30, and John 6:31-35, for example, Christ refers to himself as the fulfilment of Old Testa-ment prophecies; Romans 5:14, I Corinthians 15:20-23, and II Corinthians 3:13-14 show Christ as the fulfilment of personages or events of the Old Law, and the Epistle to the Hebrews 10:1 defines typology: 'For the law having a shadow of good things to come, and not the very image of the things can never with those sacrifices which they offered year by year continually make the comers thereunto perfect' (King James version). This definition from the book of Hebrews should be taken not as a denial of the historicity of the Old Law, or as an abrogation of the literal text. What this means in discussing typology is that in the Protestant theory of typology, as Barbara Lewalski succinctly states, 'the types con-stitute the symbolic dimension of the literal text'. [32]

Contemporaries of Bunyan show a preoccupation with typology and with the figurative elements of biblical language in order to determine the exact literal meaning with precision. Undoubtedly, the new, keenly focused Protestant emphasis upon the Word of God makes for renewed attention to the words which convey the Word. John Calvin, for example, in a section entitled 'The figurative interpretation of the decisive words' declares:

> I say that this expression is a metonymy, a figure of speech commonly used in Scripture when mysteries are under discussion. For you would not otherwise understand such expressions as 'circumcision is a covenant' [Gen. 17:13], 'the lamb is the passover' [Ex. 12:11], the sacrifices of the law are expiations [Lev. 17:11; Heb. 9:22], and finally, 'the rock from which water flowed in the desert' [Ex. 17:6], 'was Christ' [I Cor. 10:4], unless you were to take them as meanings transferred. Not only is the name transferred from something higher to something lower, but, on the other hand, the name of the visible sign is also given to the thing signified: as when God is said to have appeared to Moses in the bush [Ex. 3:2]; the Ark of the Covenant is called God and God's face [Ps. 84:8; 42:3] . . . For though the symbol differs in essence from the thing signified, (in that the latter is spiritual and heavenly, while the former is physical and visible), still, because it not only symbolizes the thing that it has been consecrated to represent as a bare and empty token but also truly exhibits it, why may its name not rightly belong to the thing? . . . those things ordained by God borrow the names of those things of which they always bear a definite and not misleading signification . . .[33]

What is significant in the lengthy statement from John Calvin is his plea that interpreters of Scripture must respond to the figurative dimensions which the literal text embodies. There is a specific meaning and there is a full and complete meaning, and both are within the literal text. To avoid misinterpretation both what the text says in its specific context and what it signifies in its figurative terms demand attention.

Similarly, William Perkins writes in his explication of Galations 4:22:

> There is but one full and intire sense of every place of scripture, and that is also the literal sense . . . To make many senses of scripture is to overturne all sense, and to make nothing certen . . .

It may be said, that the historie of Abraham's familie here pro-
pounded, hath beside his proper and literall sense, a spiritual or
mysticall sense. I answer, they are not two senses, but two parts
of one full and intire sense. For not only the bare historie, but
also that which is thereby signified, is the full sense of the
h[oly] G[host].[34]

The implication for literary study in the statements of Calvin
and Perkins has to do not with a dictation theory or with an
unimaginative reading of the text but rather a complete symbolic
reading of the types which embrace a clear and inseparable
relationship between the 'sign' and its signification. This kind of
attention to explanations of texts is John Donne's concern:

The literall sense is always to be preserved; but the literall
sense ... is not always that, which the very Letter and Grammar of
the place presents, as where it is literally said, *That Christ is a
Vine*, and literally, *That his flesh is bread* ... But the literall sense
of every place, is the principall intention of the Holy Ghost, in
that place: And his principall intention in many places, is to
express things by ... figures; so that in many places of Scripture,
a figurative sense is the literall sense.[35]

The focus of typology during the seventeenth century is another
significant aspect of the subject. It is, of course, upon Christ and
the church, but there is also a marked emphasis upon the
individual Christian. The Old Testament Temple, for example, is
foremost a type of Christ whose sacrificial death abolished the
need for the sacrifices of the Old Law; it is also a type of the Christian Church, with the Outer Court signifying the visible church,
the Holy Place typifying the invisible church on earth, and the
Holy of Holies signifying the heaven of the Saints. But the temple
also signifies the individual Christian. Joseph Hall believes so
strongly in the individual Christian as an antitype of the temple
that he says:

Where ever God dwels, there is his Temple; Oh God, thou
vouchsafest to dwell in the believing heart ... The most generall
division of the Saints is in their place and estate; some strugling,
and toyling in this earthly warfare; others truimphing in
heavenly glory; therefore hath God two other, more universall

Temples; One of the Church of his Saints on earth; the other,
the highest heaven of his Saints glorified . . . In every renewed
man, the individual temple of God; the outward parts are
allowed common to God and the world; the inwardest and sec-
retest, which is the heart, is reserved onely for the God that
made it . . .[36]

John Donne shows this thrust upon the individual of typological symbolism in his explication of David's Psalms. He urges that
the Psalms be studied 'historically, and literally . . . of David; and
. . . in their *retrospect*, as they look back upon the first *Adam*, and so
concern *Mankind collectively*, and so *you*, and I, and all have our
portion in these calamaties. . .'[37] So, then, the Psalms of David refer
to David himself, to all mankind, and to the individual. Historical
reference and typological meaning become intertwined in
Donne's statement.

If typological symbolism is of widespread concern to various
writers of the seventeenth century, so also does the subject have a
strong appeal for John Bunyan. He explains the typological
significance of Old Testament detail in several sermon-treatises,
including *The Holy City* (I, p. 295), *Solomon's Temple Spiritualized*
(III, p. 261), and *An Exposition of the first Ten Chapters of Genesis*
(III, p. 230). In one of his most sustained studies of types, the
sermon-treatise *Solomon's Temple Spiritualized*, Bunyan acknowledges that there might possibly be inaccuracies in some of the
types he explains, but he advises the reader to recognise his discovery as though 'wrapt up in a mantle, much of the glory of our
gospel matters in this temple which Solomon builded' (III, p. 221).
In several paragraphs preceding the sermon, Bunyan addresses
the reader and expresses his sheer delight in the typological symbolism of Solomon's temple: '. . . I have handled particulars one by
one, to the number of threescore and ten; namely, all of them I
could call to mind, because, as I believe, there was not one of them
but had its signification' (III, p. 221). Furthermore, he frequently
implies that figurative language is a means through which an
explicator can discern both literal and spiritual truth, as seen for
example, in the same address to the reader:

. . . many of the features of the then Church of God were set
forth, as in figures and shadows, so by places and things in that
land . . . I might also here show you, that even the gifts and

graces of the true church were set forth by the spices, nuts, pomegranates that the land of Canaan brought forth . . . But I have . . . confined myself to the immediate place of God's worship . . . (III, p. 221)

What is especially significant in Bunyan's statement for typological symbolism is that there is consideration of the literal-historical meaning of the text as an integral part of its figurative fulfilment.

In his typological treatment of Solomon's temple, Bunyan studies minutely numerous elements of the ornate temple, including where and how the temple was built, its foundation, the richness of its stones, the courts, the altar, the pillars, the porch, the doors, the mercy-seat, and various additional features.

Throughout his lengthy analysis of the text, 'Son of man show the house to the house of Israel. Show them the form of the house and its fashion; its exits and its entrances . . . and all the ordinances of it . . . and all the laws of it' (Ezek. 43:10, 11), Bunyan's figurative usage often rests on widely-accepted examples of other exegetes for whom the words of the Bible are invested with specific meaning. If he means his statement to the reader, which precedes the sermon, that he has not 'fished in other men's waters', then he is unfamiliar with comments by Christian leaders, like Calvin, for instance, or with handbooks which appeared in ever increasing numbers in the seventeenth century.[38] It is true, of course, that a discussion of types might well have been a popular topic for sermons which Bunyan heard, for as Roger Sharrock says, '. . . most of Bunyan's minor Biblical images had been anticipated in sermon treatment . . . In sermons with linked similitudes the movement from homily to symbolic narrative had already begun before the Civil War.'[39] Whatever his source, many of Bunyan's types follow traditional conceptions.

He tarries, for example, on the place, Mount Moriah, where Solomon builds the temple. It is in the 'threshing-floor of Arnon the Jebusite; whereabout Abraham offered up Isaac; there where David met the angel of the Lord, when he came with the drawn sword in his hand to cut off the people at Jerusalem, for the sin David committed in his disorderly numbering the people' (III, p. 221). Bunyan also says of Mount Moriah: 'There Abraham received his Isaac from the dead; there the Lord was entreated by David to take away the plague, and to return to Israel again in mercy; from whence, also, David gathered that there God's temple must be built' (III, p. 225). After expanding on the significance of the literal place in the Old Testament, Bunyan then declares: 'This Mount Moriah, therefore, was a type of the Son of God, the mountain of the Lord's house, the rock against which the gates of hell cannot prevail' (III, p. 225). If the mountain typifies Christ, then the stones upon which the builders erect the temple are types of the prophets and apostles; Christ is 'the foundation personally and meritoriously, but the prophets and apostles by doctrine ministerially. The Church then, which is God's New Testament temple is . . . built on Christ the foundation' (III, p. 227).

The 'outward' court receives little attention from Bunyan; it is that place 'which the people of necessity first entered, when they went to worship' (III, p. 228). But in the 'inner courts', he sees much importance: it is the place of preparation for the sin offerings, and it is in this court that the brazen altar stands. For Bunyan, the brazen altar is 'a type of Christ in his dignity. For Christ's body was our true burnt-offering, of which the bodies of the sacrificed beasts were a type' (III, p. 229).

Bunyan finds in the golden candlesticks not only beautiful ornaments but an exactness and precision shaped by the rules of the one who fashioned them; in these golden candlesticks he also finds types of the Christian Church. 'The candlestick was to hold the lights, and to show it to all the house,' says Bunyan, 'and the church is to let her light so shine that they without may see the light' (III, p. 245). When he considers the bowls and basins belonging to the temple, he sees them not as vessels in which to wash but as utensils to hold 'the messes', which the priest at the holy feasts used to set before the people who partook according to faith. Thus, they are also types of the measure of faith exercised by the individual when he comes to worship in the temple of God, his Church. To Bunyan it matters little how much nourishment is in the bowls and basins but rather how large is the bowl (the faith) of the individual who seeks nurture. 'Little bowls hold but little, nor canst thou receive, but as thy faith will bear — I speak,' he states, 'now of God's ordinary dealing with his people . . . (III, p. 251).

No study of Bunyan's *Solomon's Temple Spiritualized* is complete without attention to the office of the high priest in the inner temple. In his treatment of this most important office, however, Bunyan refers to the Tabernacle for some of his insights. To burn incense in his golden censer and to sprinkle with his finger the blood of the sacrifice upon and above the mercy seat is, according to Bunyan, the chief function of the high priest, his biblical support being Ex. XXX: 7-10 and Lev. XVI: 11-14.

For this special work, the high priest has special preparation:

> (1) He was to be washed in water; (2) Then he was to put on his holy garments; (3) After that he was to be anointed with holy oil; (4) Then an offering was to be offered for him, for the further fitting of him for his office; (5) The blood of this sacrifice must be put, some of it upon his right ear, some on the thumb of his right hand, and some on the great toe of his right foot. This done, some more of the blood, with the anointing-oil, must be sprinkled upon him and upon his garment . . . (III, p. 263)

All of this special preparation is a shadow or a type of the 'great high priest, Christ'. Each stage of the preparation is, for Bunyan, a foreshadowing of some specific feature of Christ's life and work: the working in water typifies the purity of Christ's humanity; the robes are a type of Christ's perfect righteousness; the holy oil is a figure of Christ's anointment for his work; and the sacrifices point towards the offering which Christ made of himself in the garden of Gethsemane.

To amplify his study of the office of the high priest, Bunyan goes back to Leviticus XVI and refers to Aaron's offering for the people and to his carrying the blood within the veil. He then declares:

> For Aaron was a type of Christ; his offering a type of Christ's offering his body; the blood of the sacrifice a type of the blood of Christ; his garments a type of Christ's righteousness; the mercy-seat a type of the throne of grace; the incense a type of Christ's praise; and the sprinkling of the blood of the sacrifice upon the mercy-seat a type of Christ's pleading a virtue of his sufferings for us in the presence of God in Heaven. (III, p. 263)

What Bunyan's treatment of types shows at this point is that practices, persons and events in the Old Testament typify Christ (especially his life, death and work of intercession), the Church and its apostolic, prophetic leaders as well as individual

Christians, and the spiritual state or condition of the believer.

It is futile, however, to attempt to build rigid distinctions or well-defined categories for all of Bunyan's typological symbolism. At one point in the sermon, *Solomon's Temple Spiritualized*, he stops in the midst of his various discoveries and exclaims, 'Oh, what speaking things are types, shadows, and parables, had we but eyes to see, had we but ears to hear!' (III, p. 249). It seems at times that he is overly ecstatic and that he sees the Bible invested with strange and unusual types, which are sights, sounds, and significations that belong only to his own free association. When he refers to golden nails in the temple, for example, Bunyan finds in them a type of Christ, but it is not sufficient to say as Charles Baird does that '... he reasons from the "natural" function of a nail: "a golden nail, it is to show, that as a nail, by driving is fixed in his place, so Christ by God's oath is made everlasting priest".'[40] If he reasons from the 'natural' function of a nail, and it is true that he says the nails 'were fastened to the place most holy, and of form most apt to that of which they are a figure' (III, p. 257), so also does Bunyan reason from Old Testament sources. Referring to Zechariah X: 4, he sees typological symbolism in the words: 'out of him came forth the corner, out of him the nail' (KJV), and in Ezra IX: 8, he reads, '... grace hath been *shewed* from the Lord our God ... to give us a nail in his holy place ...' (KJV). 'Now this nail in his holy place,' says Bunyan, 'is Christ, Christ ... as abiding and ever living therein for us' (III, p. 257).

The nail, as well as most of the events, personages, and objects mentioned by Bunyan have a moral or spiritual antitype. That he slights on occasion the meaning of the type as an entity in order to get before the reader the significance of the antitype or that he fails to keep his discussion of the two independent entities in balance might well be an accurate criticism of his typological symbolism. But if this is true, it is partially due to his lack of sharp distinctions among various 'similitudes', a term he frequently uses not only for types but also for figures (III, p. 257), similes (IV, p. 86), analogies (III, p. 277), exempla (II, p. 246), parables (I, p. 72), and other literary terms. Yet he specifically uses the term *type* again and again, especially in *Solomon's Temple Spiritualized*, as he speaks of literal or historical signs in the Old Testament finding their complete meaning in the New Testament antitypes. His major types are those well established in the mode of typological criticism; at the same time, this hardly means that there is complete agreement on the meaning of terms.[41] But the thoughtful words of Barbara Lewalski surely help to keep clearly in focus not only Bunyan's study of types but the whole body of knowledge called typology:

> This ... Protestant approach does not take the Bible as a multi-level allegory, but as a complex literary work whose literal meaning is revealed only by careful attention to its poetic texture and to its pervasive symbolic mode — typology. The incorporation of typological symbolism as an integral part of the literal meaning was a concomitant of the Protestant sense of the types not merely as signs or shadows pointing toward the truth to come, but as genuine symbols participating in the spiritual truth they present.[42]

Admittedly, Bunyan never declares his own view of typology as clearly as in the words of the quotation above, but his work in typology does show his love for poetic texture and for typological symbolism. He exalts types and undoubtedly would agree with Calvin that the New Testament antitypes point out 'with the finger what the law forshadowed under types'.[43]

Combined with his interest in typology as well as his concern with the structure of his sermon-treatises and preoccupation with the inherent purpose of the Book of Creatures, Bunyan evidences a fondness for additional literary features.

One of the most prevalent and most effective characteristics of Bunyan's plain prose is his use of antithesis. And one of the most pervading antitheses, which an equally pervading theme embodies, is the high dignity of man's creation versus his chosen ignoble position. The earmark of several sermons is not man's depravity but his glory. In his *Greatness of Soul*, which contains many passages of superb beauty, Bunyan shows the difference between the soul of rational man and that of the beast and in so doing stacks one on the other 'the possessions' of the soul: understanding, conscience, judgement, fancy, imagination, memory, affections, and the will; then to crown the soul's distinctiveness, he writes, 'God thought it worthy to be made, not like the earth, or the heavens, or the angels, seraphims, seraphins, or archangels, but like himself' (III, p. 160-2). 'Further,' says Bunyan 'as the soul is curious about ... every excellent thing of this life, so it is capable of having to do with invisibles, with angels . . . The soul is an intelligent power, it can be made to know and understand depths, and heights, and lengths, and breadths, in those high, sublime, and spiritual mysteries' (III, p. 168-9).

Through antithesis Bunyan enunciates the sharp contrast between the place God intended for man and the role he chose for himself:

> Man in his creation, was made in the image of God; but man, by reason of his yielding to the tempter, both made himself the very figure and image of the devil. Man, by creation, was made upright and sinless, but man, by sin, hath made himself crooked and sinful. Man, by creation, had all the faculties of his soul at liberty, to study God, his Creator, and his glorious attributes and being; but man, by sin, hath so bound up his own senses and reason, and hath given way for blindness and ignorance of God so to reign in his soul, that now he is captivated and held bound in alienation and estrangedness . . .' (I, p. 363)

Of the many short, concrete scenes in his sermon-treatises, mention should be made of Bunyan's ability to write character-sermons. In *Some Gospel Truths Opened*, for example, he sketches the profane scoffer, the formal professor, and the legal righteous. The sermon in the 'legal righteous' sketch has three principal divisions: definition, outward actions and inward revelations, and moral applications. Bunyan defines the 'legal righteous' persons as those 'ignorant of God's righteousness' who go about 'to establish their own righteousness'; their outward actions include '. . . reading, hearing sermons, prayers, public or private, peaceableness with their neighbours, fasting, alms, good works, as they count them, just dealings, abstinence from the grosser pollutions of the world, strict obedience to the commandments of the first and second table'; their inward revelation entails terse confession, 'Alas, saith one, I am a poor ignorant man, or woman; and therefore I hope the Lord will have mercy upon me' (I, p. 77). The entire sketch gives a mental picture of those 'ignorant persons' who will find no favour at the judgement.

What I.A. Richards once said in theory can be applied without forcing the point to Bunyan's panoramic 'frescoes' as well as to the little pictures: 'too much importance has been attached to the sensory qualities of images. What gives an image efficacy is less its vividness as an image than its character as a mental event.'[44] When

Bunyan depicts the predicament of a lost individual or when he portrays the profane scoffer or legal righteous or any other of his selected personalities, he invites the reader to ponder with him the experiences or the identifying characteristics of the false as well as the true pilgrim.

If the grand sketches as well as the brief ones are characteristic of Bunyan's plain prose so also is his use of repetition. Apparently for no artistic reason, on occasion he multiplies points, texts, phrases, and words, but at other times his repetitions recapitulate, summarise, and enhance the beauty of his prose. In *The Holy City* he speaks at length of the glories of the holy city and then in a summary outburst repeating the word, 'what,' he says, '. . . what a life of holiness and godliness, what dread and majesty . . . what wisdom, I say, what holiness, what grace and life, will be found . . .' (I, p. 336).

When he ponders the glory of forgiving mercy that shall show itself in that city, or when he speaks of the choirs of 'little birds' and 'pretty robins' sending forth 'their pleasant notes' to join in praising God, Bunyan shows a rich lyrical quality. Typical of his statements are:

> Our wine shall be mixed with gall no longer, we shall now drink the pure blood of the grape; the glory of pardoning and forgiving mercy shall so show itself at this day in this city, and shall so visibly abide there in the eyes of all spectators, that all shall be inflamed with it . . . Oh how clearly will all the spiders, and dragons, and owls . . . be discovered by the light thereof! Now also will all the pretty robins and little birds in the Lord's field most sweetly send their pleasant notes, and all the flowers and herbs of his garden spring. (pp. 289, 293)

The quotation cited above is a small section of a lengthy treatise, *The Holy City*, which is Bunyan's attempt to interpret the symbolism of the heavenly city described in the book of the Revelation. The work grows out of a discourse given in the prison chapel; 'while I was in the distributing of it,' he says, 'it so increased in my hand that the fragments that we left, after we had well dined, I gather up this basketfull' (I, p. 280). In referring to the lyrical tone of this work, Roger Sharrock says: 'For the first time . . . there appear virtues other than popular simplicity or proverbial flavour. There is a poetic glow about the vision which sustains it through patches of expository tedium.'[45]

If he can write with a 'poetic glow', so also is he able to express his concerns in language of satire. To discover discrepancies between appearance and reality, particularly in lives of professing believers, drives Bunyan to write with satirical barbs:

> ... feigned faith, pretended love, glorious carriages, will stand them in little stead. I call them holiday ones, for I perceive that some professors do with religion just as people do with their best apparel — hang it against the wall all the week and put it on on Sundays. For as some scarce ever put on a suit but when they go to a fair or market, so little house religion will do with some; they save religion till they go to a meeting, or till they meet with a godly chapman'. (II, p. 388)

Equally satirical are his statements aimed toward the believers who refuse to bear fruit and consequently show their hypocrisy. In *The Barren Fig-Tree*, for example,. he inveighs against the barren pretender:

> Many make religion their Cloak, and Christ their stalking-horse, and by that means cover themselves and hide their own wicked-ness from men. But God seeth their hearts, hath his print upon the heels of their feet, and pondereth all their goings; and at last ... he will either smite them with hardness of heart, and so leave them, or awaken them to bring forth fruit ... But what! Come into the pre-sence of God to sin? What! Come into the presence of God to hide thy sin? Alas, man! the church is God's garden, and Christ Jesus is the great Apostle and High-priest of our profession ... What! come into the house that is called by name — into the place where mine honour dwelleth (Ps. XXVI, 8) ... What! come there to sin, to hide thy sin, to cloke thy sin? His plants are an orchard with pleasant fruit ... And every time he goeth into his garden, it is to see the fruits of the valley ... (II, p. 251)

Another target for Bunyan's satire is the Quakers. Charles Williams says that 'Bunyan's zeal led him, in 1656, to write a book against the Quakers, entitled *Some Gospel Truths Opened*. The cham-pion on the other side was Edward Burrough. Both disputants knew more of the Saviour than of one another, and, in the fierceness of the conflict, lost sight of the obligation to think no evil.'[46] As he speaks of Christ as the 'rock' upon which a believer builds his faith, Bunyan's scathing barbs against enemies appear to justify Williams' charge: 'This is the rock . . . upon which if thou be built, the gates of hell, nor Ranter, Quaker, sin, law, death, no nor the devil himself shall ever be able to prevail against thee' (I, p. 85). Perhaps even more pointed is his statement near the close of the sermon: 'And if thou receive him in truth, then though thou do not boast, nor brag of thy holiness, as those painted hypocrites called Quakers do; yet thou wilt do more work for God in one hour, than they, even all of them, can do in their lifetime' (I, p. 86).

If he aims his sparring remarks toward religious groups, so also does Bunyan attack specific individuals. In *A Vindication of Gospel Truths Opened* (1657) he replies to Edward Burrough, spokesman for the Quakers, with even more ferociously satirical statements than in the preceding sermon. He accuses Burrough of having 'wrangled and quarrelled' (I, p. 120) but failing to give 'one plain and right answer . . .' (I, p. 120). What particularly disturbs him is Burrough's argument that an inner light dwells within every man. Specifically responding to this belief as well as to Burrough's replies in general, Bunyan declares:

> other lame arguments thou tumblest over, like a blind man in a thicket of bushes, which I pass by: but one thing more thou hast, and that is this; thou askest me 'whether I do know this light which God and Christ hath given to every man?' First, I deny that Christ, as he is mediator, hath given to every man his Spirit: and secondly, I deny that Christ, as he is God hath given to every man his Spirit; but this I say, as I have often said, it is conscience of nature itself that everyone hath . . . (I, p. 103)

What Bunyan wishes to state clearly in the sermon is that the source of spiritual discernment lies in the Triune God as the Word declares, but his convictions are not always charitably expressed. It is perhaps understandable that Henri Talon remarks of these early treatises (1656 and 1657) that 'the slightest assault from anyone seemed to him to threaten the whole kingdom of God: whence the bitterness and false sweetness of his pamphlets'.[47]

Bunyan continues to fling his satirical arrows after 1657, however, for in 1672 he writes some of his most bellicose words in *A Defence of the Doctrine of Justification by Faith in Jesus Christ*. In that year he studied a much-discussed book, *The Design of Christianity* by Edward Fowler, a Presbyterian who became an Anglican and was parish priest of Norhill in Bedfordshire. Fowler was a Doctor of Theology, an admirer of the Cambridge Platonists, and a scholar of some stature, but his credentials failed to intimidate Bunyan. 'Your book, Sir, is begun in ignorance, managed with error, and ended in blasphemy' (IV, p. 267), says Bunyan, and declares to the reader, 'Behold you here . . . a glorious Latitudinarian, that can, as to religion, turn and twist like an eel on the angle, or rather like the weathercock that stands on the steeple' (IV, p. 258). The remarks are caustic and personal, but again, Bunyan sincerely believes that Fowler deliberately attempts to minimise the justification which Christ provides for one who believes by faith. To Fowler, the doctrine of justification by faith should command little attention. What matters to him is a belief in the purity of human nature which Christ originally placed in the soul, and it was to restore this uncorrupted holiness that Christ had died. In his coming to earth, Christ offered himself primarily as a model for living, not as a Redeemer in whom repentant sinners should and could call upon in faith. Such thinking causes Bunyan to strike out violently: 'These are but words; there is no such thing as purity of our nature, abstract and distinct from the sinful pollution that dwelleth in us' (IV, p. 222).

For more than 45 pages Bunyan directs his shafts against Edward Fowler and his book, *The Design of Christianity*. At times his remarks appear overstated, but faith is of immense importance to Bunyan, and for anyone to give the slightest impression of undermining such a worthy principle is simply more than he can tolerate. Admittedly, there is a rough texture in his prose, but Sharrock's insights are helpful on sermons containing heated satire: 'the rough texture . . . is lightened by passionate conviction, by imagination . . . and above all by a fund of realistic imagery drawn from the life of the people'.[48]

In some works, he speaks beautifully of faith. In *Christian Behaviour*, for example, he says: '. . . faith is a principle of life by which a Christian lives . . . a principle of strength by which the soul opposeth . . . this world' (II, p. 165). Later, in the same work, he states: 'Faith is so great an artist in arguing and reasoning with the soul, that it will bring over the hardest heart that it hath to deal with . . . it will show me that God will have me an heir of glory' (II, p. 166).

If he can show the joy and power of faith, Bunyan is also able to offer comfort and hope to the believer. Drawing on the harmonious prose from the book of Ecclesiastes, he speaks of the importance of right timing and says: 'There is a time to pray, a time to hear, a time to read, a time to confer, a time to meditate, a time to do, and a time to suffer' (II, p. 168). Equally joyous and beautiful are the lines in *Come and Welcome to Jesus Christ*, adapted from the Song of Songs:'. . . Christ inviteth thee to dine and sup with him; he inviteth thee to a banquet of wine, yea to come into his wine-cellar, and his banner over thee shall be love' (II, p. 227).

From these two statements quoted above it is obvious that Bunyan transposes some of his citations from Scripture. As Barbara Lewalski suggests, '. . . a large number of moderate Anglicans and Puritans [of the seventeeth century] . . . took the scriptures to be unsurpassed in eloquence and power to move and persuade'.[49] Bunyan himself holds, as we have earlier stated, that the language of Scripture embodies truth, that literary features should be studied, not ignored, and that Old Testament and New Testament writers and Christ himself validate literary forms. Furthermore, Bunyan needs no persuasion regarding the plentitude of literary figures in Scripture and has no hesitancy concerning the appropriation of a remarkable variety in his sermons. Of all literary figures, however, the simile has a special appeal for Bunyan as well as for other writers.

Robert Cawdrey wrote an excellent book entitled *Treasurie or Store-House of Similies*[50] in which he cites similes from the Bible and builds the same figure based on scriptural texts. No reader of Bunyan finds surprise, however, that Cawdrey discovers a tremendous array of similes from every facet of the natural world which illumine spiritual matters. For instance, Bunyan remarks: 'Zeal without knowledge is like a mettled horse without eyes, or like a sword in a madman's hand' (II, p. 168), or, 'Faith dissolves doubts, as the sun drives away the mists' (II, p. 482), or '. . . there are some professors do not go so fast in the way of God as a snail doth go on the wall . . .' (IV, p. 177), or,

> When God hath thus appeared in the glory of his grace, and the glory of his power, to deliver his chosen, then shall the implacable enemies of God shrink and creep into holes, like the locusts and frogs, of the hedges, at the appearance of the glory of the majesty of God. (I, p. 290)

At times Bunyan uses a series of similes, as in *The Holy City*, when he compares the glories of the New Jerusalem with the world in that day when all spiritual riches are removed from it.

> Wherefore the rest of the world at this day will be but as a crushed bunch of herbs in which is no virtue; or like a furnace full of dross, out of which the gold is taken; or like an old crazy and ruinous house, from which is departed all health and happiness; and indeed ... at this day the whole circumference of the world that is without the walls and privileges of this city, it shall be but like an old ruinous house, in which dwells nothing but cormorants, bitterns, owls, ravens, dragons, satyrs, the screech-owl, the great owl, the vulture and the like most doleful birds. (I, p. 311)

What Joan Webber says of *Grace Abounding* is perhaps true of Bunyan's sermons: 'Simile is a simple way of controlling the imagination, and it is analogous here to the habit of breaking apart generalization and concrete detail ... If you say one thing is like another, you can keep the two distinct and unconfused in your mind more easily than if you fuse them into metaphor.'[51]

It is unwise, however, to infer from Webber's statement that Bunyan is unable to write in metaphors. He calls Satan, for example, the 'merciless butcher of men' (I, p. 65). The Son of God is 'the Captain-general of the saints' (I, p. 292), and Christ is 'the door to God' (I, p. 303) and 'captain-general of all the forces that God hath in heaven and earth, the king and commander of his people' (IV, p. 349). He further states that Christ rising from the dead is 'the sheaf of first fruits' (IV, p. 215), and declares that a broken heart is 'the handiwork of God' (III, p.356). Perhaps one of the most traditional metaphors used by John Bunyan is the 'glass of the Word'. Writers frequently appropriate the metaphor as a way of perceiving a new understanding of God and of man. John Donne, for example, speaks of the glass of Scripture as the clearest route to apprehending God:

> The blindest man that is, hath the face of God so turned towards him, as that he may be seen by him; even the *naturall man* hath so; for, therefore does the Apostle make him inexcusable, if in the visible worke, he doe not see the *invisible* God. But all sight of God, is by the benefit of a *law*; the naturall man sees him by a law written in his *heart, the Jew*, by a law given by

Moses, the Christian, in a clearer glasse, for, his law is the Gospell. (X, p. 108)

In his sermon, *The Excellency of a Broken Heart*, Bunyan says of the man whose heart is contrite and broken: 'He finds by nature no form nor comeliness in himself; but the more he looks in the glass of the word, the more unhandsome, the more deformed he perceiveth sin has made him' (III, p. 345).

Another literary figure which he undoubtedly finds extremely helpful in emphasising scriptural truth is anaphora; in referring to the parable from Luke XVI: 19-31 and particularly to the statement, 'But Abraham said, Son, remember . . .' Bunyan says in *Sighs from Hell*: '. . . Thou art now sensible what it is to lose thy soul, thou art now sensible what it is to put off repentance; thou art now sensible that thou hast befooled thyself . . .' (I, p. 146). What the relation of the Christian is to law may be seen in this anaphora from *The Holy City*: 'The law commands right obedience, and the Christian giveth it; the law commands continual obedience, and the Christian giveth it' (I, p. 305). Conversely, to show the multifaceted power of grace, Bunyan says in *The Saint's Privilege and Profit*: 'It is grace that chooses, it is grace that calleth, it is grace that preserveth, and it is grace that brings to glory: even the grace that like a river of water of life proceedeth from this throne' (IV, p. 281).

With powerful effect Bunyan is able on occasion to fuse anaphora with antithesis in order to show the sharp difference between what *is* and what *ought to be*. In *The Resurrection of the Dead*, he declares:

> Man, in his creation, was made in the image of God; but man, by reason of his yielding to the tempter, hath made himself the very figure and image of the devil. Man, by creation, was made upright and sinless; but man by sin, hath made himself crooked and sinful. Man, by creation, has all the faculties of his soul at liberty, to study God, his Creator, and his glorious attributes and being; but man, by sin, hath so bound up his own senses and reason, and hath given way for blindness and ignorance of God so to reign in his soul, that now he is captivated, and held bound in alienation . . . both from God and all things spiritually good . . . (I, p. 363)

If, as Henri Talon suggests, Bunyan makes use of all the formulas which help the memory,[52] then his homely proverbs must also be included among the characteristic features of the sermons. In speaking of the shallow lives of some Christians, he says: '. . . we are a company of worn-out Christians; our moon is in the wane; we are much more black than white, more dark than light; we shine but a little . . .' (II, p. 470). With terseness, he also remarks, 'Religion to most men, is but a by-business, with which they fill up spare hours . . .' (III, p. 462) or, 'Profess men may, and make a noise, as the empty barrel maketh the biggest sound . . .' (III, p. 365). In referring to man's poverty without Christ, Bunyan declares: 'There is none has spiritual gold to sell but Christ' (III, p. 348). Professing Christians, who lack dedication, Bunyan calls 'holiday ones', and, as stated earlier, he perceives '. . . that some professors do with religion just as people do with their best apparel, hang it against the wall all week, and put it on on Sundays' (II, p. 388).

If he appropriates the proverbs that lodge in the memory, so also does Bunyan write sermon-treatises that encompass the human senses. In *The Acceptable Sacrifice; or the Excellency of a Broken Heart*, he shows in five sequential paragraphs the ways in which a broken-hearted man exercises his senses (III, p. 344-5). *The Greatness of Soul* also shows in five paragraphs the manner in which the soul, as well as the body, sees, hears, tastes, smells, and feels (III, p. 162-3). What is of especial interest in his depiction of the place of the senses is the absence of any scale of gradation. To Bunyan each of the senses seems to be equally important, even though it is obvious in many of his sermons that he emphasises his belief that faith comes by hearing. There also prevails the view that sharp definitions between the believer's senses and those of the carnal minded may be ill-founded. In *The Greatness of Soul*, for example, he declares:

> As . . . the body can see beasts, trees, men, and all visible things, so the soul can see God, Christ, angels, heaven, devils, hell, and other things that are invisible; nor is this property peculiar only to the souls that are illuminated by the Holy Ghost, for the most casual soul in the world shall have a time to see these things, but not to its comfort, but not to its joy, but to its endless woe and misery . . . (III, p. 162)

With Bunyan, any distinction lies in what one sees, not in the capacity for seeing.

What is of further interest is that images of the senses capture the imagination of theologians and ministers far more formally educated than John Bunyan. In one of his sermons, John Donne, for example, seems to give a special place to seeing or to sight imagery:

> Darkness is that, by which the Holy Ghost himselfe hath chosen to expresse *hell*; hell is *darkness*; and the way to it, to hell is *Excaecation* in this life, blindness in our spirituall eyes. Eternall life hereafter is *Visio Dei*, the sight of God, and the way to that here, is to *see God* here. (IV, p. 173)

For Donne, however, there is something of a hierarchy among the senses. As Winfried Schleiner remarks '. . . Donne knows, and repeats several times, that faith comes through hearing . . . But there is an element of incompleteness about this sense: hearing is good and necessary, but seeing is better.'[53] Yet, both Bunyan and Donne perceive through images the capacity of sin to blur or to mar spiritual vision, a concern frequently expressed in homiletic literature.

To make his sermons clearer and more vivid to his countrymen, many of whom had no artistic preoccupation, Bunyan also finds in the anecdote yet one more way of calling attention to truth. In *Jerusalem Sinner Saved; or Good News for the Vilest of Men*, for example, he remarks:

> I heard a story from a soldier, who with his company had laid siege against a fort, that so long as the besieged were persuaded their foes would show them no favour, they fought like madmen; but when they saw one of their fellows taken, and received to favour, they all came tumbling down from their fortress, and delivered themselves into their enemies' hands. (II, p. 465)

Bunyan immediately makes his moral application: 'I am persuaded, did men believe that there is that grace and willingness in the heart of Christ to save sinners, as the word imports there is, they would come tumbling into his arms; but Satan has blinded their minds, that they cannot see this thing' (II, p. 465).

The rhetorical question, a device Bunyan frequently appropriates to arouse the attention of his audience, threads throughout numerous sermons. To lure tempted individuals to focus on their

privileges rather than on their testings, he says in *The Saint's
Privilege and Profit*:

> Behold, tempted soul, dost thou yet see what a throne of grace
> here is, and what multitudes are already arrived thither to give
> thanks unto his name that sits thereon . . .? And wilt thou hang
> thy harp upon the willow, and go drooping up and down the
> world, as if there was no God, no grace, no throne of grace to
> apply thyself unto, for mercy and grace to help in time of need . . .
> Or is his grace so far gone, and so near spent, that now he has
> not enough to pardon and secure, and save one sinner more?
> (IV, p. 283)

Single, individual words frequently offer to one's contemplation
an image of painful immediacy. Obviously finding the participle
of singular significance in depicting the agony of the damned soul,
Bunyan says: 'There they shall be ever *whining, pining, weeping,
mourning* . . .' (I, p. 150). To show the mighty impact of God's presence on a human heart, he contends that it manifests itself in one
of two ways: 'a *trembling* . . . and *quailing* of heart or else a *buckling*
and *bending* of heart . . .' (I, p. 290).

Closely aligned to the rhetorical question is his remarkable
dialogue. 'No matter what sermon we glance at,' says Talon, 'we
shall be sure to find self-with-self dialogue.'[54] His mind and his
heart are often in conflict. In considering what condition despair
is capable of bringing to his own soul, he debates with self:

> . . . O my soul! this is not the place of despair; this is not the time
> to despair in. As long as mine eyes can find a promise in the
> Bible, as long as there is the least mention of grace, as long as
> there is a moment left me of breath or life in this world, so long
> will I wait or look for mercy, so long will I fight against unbelief
> and despair. (II, p. 478)

If the self-with-self dialogue is present so also is the dialogue
with another individual, though the other is invisible. On the same
subject of despair, he forcefully declares:

> Despair! When we have a God of mercy and a redeeming Christ
> alive! For shame, forbear; let them despair that dwell where
> there is no God . . . A living man despair . . ! Oh! so long as we are

where promises swarm, where mercy is proclaimed, where grace reigns ... it is a base thing to despair. (II, p. 478)

In his sermons, Bunyan obviously accomplishes through dialogue what James Thorpe perceives in *Grace Abounding* and *The Pilgrim's Progress*: 'He developed dialogue which could present the inner world of the mind as well as the outer world of language and action.'[55]

What becomes especially clear in a study of Bunyan's literary practices is that there is hardly a conceivable literary device that he fails to appropriate in his sermon-treatises. He thinks of each of these as yet another embodiment of truth as he sincerely desires to depict it. He also knows how to select literary features that his audience could appreciate. Perhaps there is no more vivid illustration of his concern for those to whom he speaks than in his sermon-treatise, *The Holy City*, especially in the statement:

You know it is usual for the Holy Ghost in Scriptures to call the saints, sheep, lambs, heifers, cows, rams, doves, swallows, pelicans, and the like; and also to call their food, their spiritual and heavenly food, grass, provender, wheat, wine, oil, grapes, apples, figs, nuts, and the like also; all which are but shadowish ... expressions even as this of the measure of the twelve thousand furlongs. And observe it, that which John saith here is twelve thousand furlongs, Ezekiel tells us lieth on this side and on that side of the bank of the river of the water of life. (I, p. 306)[57]

Bunyan's prose is that of common speech, 'the colloquial rhythms', as Joan Webber says, 'of man speaking to men'.[56] At times, some literary features show a crudity not seen in the more formally trained preachers of his century, but it is still a happy fact that he creates through them powerful effects.

Notes

1. Augustine, *On Christian Doctrine*, trans. D.W. Robertson Jr. (Indianapolis and New York, 1958), p. 121.

2. See D.W. Robertson Jr., 'Translator's Introduction' in *On Christian Doctrine*, pp. ix-xii for further discussion of Augustine's exegetical principles and the influence of *On Christian Doctrine* during the Middle Ages and in subsequent eras.

3. Barbara Reynolds gives an excellent discussion of the fourfold interpretation as Dante views it in 'Introduction' to 'Paradise', *The Divine Comedy* (Baltimore, 1976), pp. 44-9.

4. This is the biblical passage in which Dante professes to discover the four levels of interpretation about which he writes in his alleged *Epistle to Can Grande*.

5. American Standard Version of The Holy Bible.

6. Perkins, *The Arte of Prophecying. Or, A Treatise Concerning the Sacred and Onely True Manner and Methode of Preaching*, trans. Thomas Tuke, *Workes*, 3 vols. (London, 1612-1613), *II*, 646.

7. Among the manuals for preachers were: William Chapell, *The Preacher of the Art and Method of Preaching* (London, 1656), and John Wilkins, *Ecclesiastes, or, A Discourse Concerning the Gift of Preaching As It Falls Under the Rules of Art* (London, 1646).

8. Barbara Lewalski, *Protestant Poetics and the Seventeenth-Century Religious Lyric* (Princeton, 1979), p. 219.

9. Joseph Glanvill, *Essays Concerning Preaching; Written for the Direction of a Young Divine* . . . (London, 1703), p. 46.

10. Henri Talon, *John Bunyan The Man and His Works* (Cambridge, Mass., 1951), p. 112.

11. Quotations from John Donne's sermons are from *The Sermons of John Donne*, 10 vols., ed. George R. Potter and Evelyn M. Simpson (Berkeley, 1953-62).

12. Ibid., II, 170-1.

13. See Lewalski's reference to moderate Anglicans and Puritans, p. 222.

14. Quoted by Douglas Bush, *English Literature in the Seventeenth Century*, 2nd edn (Oxford, 1962), p. 328.

15. *The Works of George Herbert*, ed. F.E. Hutchinson (Oxford, 1941), pp. 233-4, 257.

16. Ibid., pp. 234-5.

17. Wilkins, *Ecclesiastes, or, a Discourse Concerning the Gift of Preaching As it Falls Under the Rules of Art*, p. 128.

18. South, *Sermons Preached upon Several Occasions* (Oxford, 1823), IV, 149-51.

19. Greaves, *John Bunyan* (Grand Rapids, 1969), p. 61.

20. For a scholarly study of the place of metaphor during the Middle Ages, see Ernst Curtius, *European Literature and the Latin Middle Ages*, trans. William R. Trask (New York, 1953).

21. Donne, *Sermons*, IV, 167.

22. Donne, *Sermons*, IX, 236.

23. Calvin, *Institutes*, ed. John T. McNeill, 2 vols. *Library of Christian Classics* (Philadelphia, 1960), *I*, 52-3. 62.

24. Ibid., pp. 179-80.

25. Donne, *Sermons*, VI, 143.

26. Richard Baxter, *A Christian Divinity: Or, A Sermon of Practical Theologie* (London, 1673), p. 301.

27. Joseph Hall, *Arte of Divine Meditation* (London, 1607), pp. 16-17.

28. Robert Boyle, *Occasional Reflections upon Several Subjects, Whereto is premis'd A Discourse about such kind of Thoughts* (London, 1665), p. 19.

29. Lewalski, *Protestant Poetics and the Seventeenth-Century Religious Lyric*, p. 162.

30. Sir Thomas Browne, 'Religio Medici', *The Major Works*, ed. C.A. Patrides (New York, 1977), p. 153.

31. For further study see J.S. Preuss, *From Shadow to Promise: Old Testament Interpretation from Augustine to Young Luther* (Cambridge, Mass., 1969); Victor Harris, 'Allegory to Analogy in the Interpretation of Scriptures', *PQ*, *45* (1966), 1-23; Sacvan Bercovitch, 'Typology in Puritan New England: The Williams-Cotton Controversy Reassessed', *AQ*, *19* (1967), 166-91.

32. Lewalski, *Protestant Poetics and the Seventeenth-Century Religious Lyric*, p. 123.

33. Calvin, *Institutes*, ed. McNeill, IV, 1385.

34. Perkins, *A Commentarie Exposition upon the Five First Chapters of the Epistle to the Galatians* (Cambridge, 1604), p. 346.

35. Donne, *Sermons*, VI, 62.

36. Hall, *Contemplations upon the Principall Passages of the holy Storie*, *Works*, 3 vols. (London, 1628-34), II, 1220-2.

37. Donne, *Sermons*, II, 75.

38. William Guild, *Moses Unveiled; or, those figures which served unto the patterne and shadow of heavenly things, pointing out the Messiah Christ Revealed, or The Old Testament Explained* (London, 1635); Henry Vertue, *Christ and the Church, or Parallels* (London, 1659); Benjamin Keach, *Tropologia: A Key to open Scripture Metaphors . . . Together with Types of the Old Testament* (London, 1681); Samuel Mather, *The Figure or types of the Old Testament* (Dublin, 1683).

39. Sharrock, *John Bunyan* (London, 1954), p. 96.

40. Baird, *John Bunyan. A Study in Narrative Technique* (Port Washington, NY, 1977), p. 19.

41. Richard Douglas Jordan, *The Temple of Eternity* (Port Washington, NY, 1972), p. 59, expresses uneasiness with what he believes to be simple statements on typology. He says, for instance, ' "Typology" ', says Jean Danielow, "is the study of correspondences between the Old and the New Testaments." [See *The Lord of History*.] Were it only as simple as that statement makes it seem. For hundreds of years, Christian writers have argued about what "parallels" are and are not types. For three hundred years, at least, theologians have attempted to make a distinction between true types and those which are the products of allegorizing.'

42. Lewalski, *Donne's Anniversaries* (Princeton, 1973), pp. 154-5.

43. Calvin, *Institutes*, ed. McNeill, I, 426.

44. I.A. Richards, *Principles of Literary Criticism* (London, 1925), p. 119.

45. Sharrock, *John Bunyan The Man and His Works*, p. 45.

46. Charles Williams, *A Bi-Centenary of John Bunyan* (London, n.d.), p. 45.

47. Talon, *John Bunyan*, p. 95.

48. Sharrock, *John Bunyan*, pp. 52-3.

49. Lewalski, *Protestant Poetics and the Seventeenth-Century Religious Lyric*, p.222.

50. Robert Cawdrey, *A Treasurie or Store-House of Similies* (London, 1600).

51. Joan Webber, *The Eloquent 'I'* (Madison, 1968), p. 45.

52. Talon, *John Bunyan The Man and His Works*, p. 128.

53. Winfried Schleiner, *The Imagery of John Donne's Sermons* (Providence, 1970), p. 154.

54. Talon, *John Bunyan The Man and His Works*, p. 128.

55. James Thorpe, 'Introduction', *The Pilgrim's Progress and Grace Abounding* (New York, 1969), p. xxi.

56. Webber, *The Eloquent 'I'*, p. 38.

57. All quotations for the serman-treatise are from *The Entire Works of John Bunyan*, ed. Henry Stebbings, 4 vols. (London, 1862).

8 CONCLUSION

A study of John Bunyan's imaginative works clearly indicates that his obvious preoccupation with moral and theological teaching does not erase his concern for literary art. His writings show his interest in structure, generic form, and other features of imaginative literature. That he is a conscientious believer who desires to direct his writings toward religious ends is subject to no debate; that he believes in story and leads the reader to search out dimensions not apparent in the configuration of images, characters, and scenes is equally incontrovertible. Allusive metaphorical language challenges the critic-reader to discover new meanings and to see the familiar in a new way. Whether he works as a writer conscious of literary art is no easy question to settle regarding him or any author, but it is a certainty that Bunyan's theoretical understanding of fictional writing as well as his accomplishments as a writer of imaginative literature and as a shaper of sermons suggest a perception not always admitted by Bunyan's critics. He may sometimes in his art have produced more, or less, than was his conscious intention, but evidence of a vivid imagination pervades his works.

In *Grace Abounding, The Pilgrim's Progress* (Parts One and Two), *The Life and Death of Mr. Badman, The Holy War*, and the *Emblems*, Bunyan shows an ordering of language dealing with elemental human experience and a unified form and content with a thematic structure, not a series of moral and theological episodes masquerading as literary art. Throughout all of his works, however, there is a clear design that points towards the spiritual by means of the literal, for the allusiveness in his works depends on a body of belief to which he unequivocally commits himself.

Grace Abounding exhibits features characteristic of Bunyan's best dialogue, the struggles of one central character are unfolded in an essentially dramatic way; interior monologues and dialogues, images of torture, agony, and doubt, attain the force of immediacy in his remembrance of the past.

The Pilgrim's Progress intensively and extensively explores both inner and outer aspects of a pilgrim's journey. The various stages disclose the presence of characteristic features of allegory: the idea and the image, the pilgrimage, the dream phenomenon, and the 'debates' or dialogue. Each allegorical scene, through contrast or metaphor — such as the metaphor of sight, or by alluding to external places, things, or conditions, explores and probes the intense conflicts of the major characters. Through images, the work brings into play a conception of a moral order implicit in the universe, and the actions debate or portray man's profound spiritual dilemmas.

Although *The Life and Death of Mr. Badman* lacks the universality of *The Pilgrim's Progress*, it clearly reveals through dialogue two clearly differentiated male characters and one female individual, Mrs Badman. Primarily, the unfolding of the life of Badman is a preparation for the account of his death. But the various stories and anecdotes, told to portray Badman, have a dramatic effect of their own in their immediacy and, frequently, in their vivid horror.

The Holy War with its intricate levels of allegory and its long, formal scenes defines the nature of man's soul in terms of two warring, antagonistic powers. In its epic-like structure, which shifts from earth to heaven, to hell, to battle fields, and into the inner thoughts of individuals, the allegory shows a thematic unity in the continuous warfare between God and Satan for man's soul. Various kinds of contrast, 'character-writing', parody, imagery, and lively dialogue all combine to depict the unfolding action.

Allusiveness in the *Emblems*, as well as emblematic passages found in various works, depends upon the author's commitment to the belief in a divine order. Objects and events in the natural world are emblems of spiritual matters. A stalk of grain, a flock of birds, a hive of bees, a spider in a web and all created things are charged with significant meaning and are analogous to transcendent, spiritual truths.

The structure of his sermons discloses awareness of various seventeenth-century models for sermons, but Bunyan does not restrict his structure merely to familiar patterns. He organises at times around one central figure or works out an allegory around a parable or constructs questions and answers. Occasionally, he builds treatises on familiar concepts; less frequently, he organises sermons around several passages of Scripture from a given chapter or even one word. Whatever his mode of construction, Bunyan shows widely-ranged patterns of structure.

Not only in the Book of the Word but also in the book of the world or of creatures does he find a vast field for interpretative materials. To neglect the book of creatures is to ignore manifestations of God as well as moral and spiritual lessons for man.

In the symbolism of typology, Bunyan demonstrates his variant of the Protestant theory of typology, widely accepted in the seventeenth century. Numerous sermons indicate his belief that types are symbolic dimensions of the literal text, and that typology, a mode practised by Patristic, medieval, and seventeenth-century exegetes, pertains to Old Testament persons, events, ceremonies, and artefacts which are fulfilled in the New Testament.

Careful study of the prose treatises also shows Bunyan's ability to handle artistically a wide range of literary terms, including antithesis, repetition, satire, simile, metaphor, and others. What is unquestionably clear, as indicated earlier, is that there is hardly a conceivable literary device that he fails to appropriate in his sermon-treatises. Equally clear is Bunyan's depiction of these as an embodiment of truth as he sincerely desires to disclose it.

Whatever the strengths or the weaknesses of his literary ways, Bunyan fully pursues the form in which he chooses to write. Whatever judgements are made on his method, they must be made in terms of the method he pursued in his age, not in terms of other forms or other methods used by writers in other ages.

In this study my primary concern has been not to defend Bunyan's literary art but rather to call attention to the qualities which characterise writings which have survived for three centuries. Those features will surely aid in telling on their own merit a more complete story of Bunyan as an imaginative writer.

SELECT BIBLIOGRAPHY

Rather than list a bibliography of the scores of books and essays consulted and studied for this book, I should like to recommend a few works for all readers of Bunyan.

Primary Sources

Buchanan, E.S. (ed.) John Bunyan, *A Book for Boys and Girls* or *Country Rhymes for Children* (American Tract Society, New York, 1928)

Forrest, James F. (ed.) *The Holy War* (New York University Press, New York, 1967)

The Miscellaneous Works of John Bunyan (Oxford University Press, New York, 1976). Thirteen volumes projected

Offor, G. *The Works of John Bunyan*, 3 vols. (Blackie and Son, Glasgow, 1858-9

Sharrock, Roger (ed.) *Grace Abounding to the Chief of Sinners and The Pilgrim's Progress* (Oxford University Press, London, 1966)

Stebbing, H. *The Entire Works of John Bunyan*, 4 vols. (James S. Virtue, London 1859-60)

Wharey, J. Blanton (ed.) *The Pilgrim's Progress*, 2nd edn, revised by Roger Sharrock (Clarendon Press, Oxford, 1960)

Secondary Sources

Alpaugh, David. 'Emblem and Interpretation in *The Pilgrim's Progress*', *ELH, 33* (1966), pp. 200-314

Baird, Charles W. *John Bunyan A Study in Narrative Technique* (Kennikat Press, Port Washington, NY, 1977)

Beal, Rebecca. 'Grace Abounding to the Chief of Sinners: John Bunyan's Pauline Epistle', *SEL* 21 (1981), pp. 148-60

Daly, Peter. *Literature in the Light of the Emblem* (University of Toronto Press, Toronto, 1979)

Firth, Charles H. 'Bunyan's Holy War', *The Journal of English*

Studies, 1 (1913), pp. 141-50

Fish, Stanley Eugene. 'Progress in *The Pilgrim's Progress*' in *Self-Consuming Artifacts: The Experience of Seventeenth-Century Literature* (University of California Press, Berkeley, 1972), pp. 224-64

Forrest, James F. 'Introduction', *The Holy War* (New York University Press, New York, 1967)

Freeman, Rosemary. *English Emblem Books* (Chatto and Windus, London, 1948)

Frye, Roland Mushat. 'Pilgrim's Progress and the Christian Life', *God, Man and Satan: Patterns of Christian Thought in Paradise Lost, The Pilgrim's Progress, and the Great Theologians* (Princeton University Press, Princeton, 1960), pp. 95-167

Greaves, Robert L. *John Bunyan* (William B. Eerdmans' Publishing Company, Grand Rapids, 1969)

Harrison, G.B. *John Bunyan, A Study in Personality* (J.M. Dent and Sons, London, 1928)

Kaufman, U. Milo. *The Pilgrim's Progress and Traditions in Puritan Meditation* (Yale University Press, New Haven, 1966)

Knott, John R., Jr 'Bunyan's Gospel Day: A Reading of *The Pilgrim's Progress*', *English Literary Renaissance, 3* (1973), pp. 443-61

—— 'Bunyan and the Holy Community', *SP*, LXXX, no. 2 (Spring, 1983), pp. 200-25

Lowes, John Livingston. '*The Pilgrim's Progress*: A Study in Literary Immortality', Essays in Appreciation (The Riverside Press, Cambridge, Mass., 1936), pp. 35-74

Newey, Vincent (ed.) *The Pilgrim's Progress* (Liverpool University Press, Liverpool, 1980)

Sadler, Lynn Veach, *John Bunyan* (Twayne Publishers, Boston, 1979)

Sharrock, Roger, *John Bunyan* (Hutchinson House, London, 1954)

—— 'Personal Vision and Puritan Tradition in Bunyan', *The Hibbert Journal, 56* (1957), pp. 47-60

—— 'Bunyan and the English Emblem Writers'. Review of English Studies, *21* (1945), pp. 105-16

Stranahan, Brainerd P. 'Bunyan's Special Talent: Biblical Texts as "Events" in *Grace Abounding* and *The Pilgrim's Progress*', *ELR*, 11 (1981), pp. 329-43

Talon, Henri A. *John Bunyan The Man and His Works*, trans. Mrs

Bernard Wall (Harvard University Press, Cambridge, 1951)

Tyndall, William York, *John Bunyan Mechanick Preacher* (Russell and Russell, New York, 1934)

Tuve, Rosamond. *Allegorical Imagery: Some Medieval Books and Their Posterity* (Princeton University Press, Princeton, 1966)

Watson, Melvin, 'The Drama of Grace Abounding', *English Studies, 46* (December 1969), pp. 471-82

Webber, Joan. *The Eloquent 'I': Style and Self in Seventeenth-Century Prose* (University of Wisconsin Press, Madison, 1968)

INDEX

L